The Emotionally
Troubled Adolescent
and the
Family Physician

The Emotionally Troubled Adolescent and the Family Physician

143570

Edited By

MICHAEL G. KALOGERAKIS, M.D.

Clinical Associate Professor of Psychiatry
New York University School of Medicine
Chief, Inpatient Adolescent Service
Bellevue Psychiatric Hospital

RJ503
E47

CHARLES C THOMAS · PUBLISHER
Springfield · Illinois · U.S.A.

Published and Distributed Throughout the World by
CHARLES C THOMAS • PUBLISHER
BANNERSTONE HOUSE
301-327 East Lawrence Avenue, Springfield, Illinois, U.S.A.

© *1973, by* CHARLES C THOMAS • PUBLISHER
ISBN 0-398-02844-3
Library of Congress Catalog Card Number: 73-4019

With THOMAS BOOKS *careful attention is given to all details of manufacturing and design. It is the Publisher's desire to present books that are satisfactory as to their physical qualities and artistic possibilities and appropriate for their particular use. THOMAS BOOKS will be true to those laws of quality that assure a good name and good will.*

Library of Congress Cataloging in Publication Data
The Emotionally troubled adolescent and the family physician.

Includes papers presented at a panel organized by the American Society for Adolescent Psychiatry at the annual convention of the American Medical Association.
    1. Adolescent psychiatry—Congresses. 2. Adolescence—Congresses. I. Kalogerakis, Michael G., ed. II. American Society for Adolescent Psychiatry. [DNLM: 1. Adolescent psychology—Congresses. 2. General practice—Congresses. WS 462 E54 1973]
RJ503.E47   616.8'9   73-4019
ISBN 0-398-02844-3

Printed in the United States of America
N-1

CONTRIBUTORS

ROBERT E. GOULD, M.D.

Associate Professor of Clinical Psychiatry
New York University School of Medicine
Director of Adolescent Services
Bellevue Psychiatric Hospital
New York City, New York

ADELE D. HOFMANN, M.D.

Assistant Professor of Clinical Pediatrics
New York University School of Medicine
Director of the Adolescent Medical Unit
Department of Pediatrics
Bellevue Hospital
New York City, New York

MICHAEL G. KALOGERAKIS, M.D.

Clinical Associate Professor of Psychiatry
New York University School of Medicine
Chief, Inpatient Adolescent Service
Bellevue Psychiatric Hospital
New York City, New York

MALVINA W. KREMER, M.D.

Clinical Associate Professor of Psychiatry
New York University School of Medicine
New York City, New York;
Supervising and Training Analyst,
Comprehensive Course in Psychoanalysis,
N.Y. Medical College

SAMUEL SLIPP, M.D.

Clinical Associate Professor of Psychiatry
New York University School of Medicine
Head of Family & Group Therapy Program
Bellevue Psychiatric Hospital
New York City, New York

v

ALEXANDRA SYMONDS, M.D.

Clinical Assistant Professor of Psychiatry
New York University School of Medicine
Consulting Psychoanalyst to the Young Adult Program
Karen Horney Clinic
New York City, New York

MARTIN SYMONDS, M.D.

Clinical Associate Professor of Psychiatry
New York University School of Medicine
New York City, New York

JOSEPH D. TEICHER, M.D.

Professor of Psychiatry
University of Southern California
Los Angeles, California

JAMES M. TOOLAN, M.D.

Assistant Professor of Clinical Psychiatry
University of Vermont, College of Medicine
Medical Director
United Counseling Service of Bennington County, Vermont
Old Bennington, Vermont

PREFACE

THIS LITTLE VOLUME first began to take form as a panel organized by the American Society for Adolescent Psychiatry at the Annual Convention of the American Medical Association. The thought then was to bring the experience of established adolescent psychiatrists to the general physician faced with troubled teen-age patients. There was general agreement that they posed special problems, requiring particular handling. Knowledge of their world, their style and their concerns seemed more essential to working with them than was the case with either adults or children. They were often taxing and testy and many a practitioner would sooner let his younger colleague sharpen his clinical skills on the adolescent than handle it himself.

The panel stirred considerable interest, and was well-attended, indicating that a real need for more information about adolescent problems and their management existed among non-psychiatrists in the medical profession. It was a natural step to consider expanding on the material covered by the panel by adding a few contributions on uncovered subjects and publishing.

Of major importance in the initial conceptualization of the panel and, subsequently, in the idea for the book, are two related facts. First, the serious shortage of psychiatric manpower in the face of an ever-growing need and, secondly, the established ability of many physicians lacking extensive exposure to psychiatry to deal effectively with many of the emotional problems they encounter routinely in their office practice.

What has been gathered together to create this book are the excellent papers presented at the panel (S. Slipp, A. & M. Symonds, M. Kremer), and others written expressly for the book. An effort has been made to maintain high quality and comprehensiveness in the individual contributions. The authors are authorities in the area they have chosen to address.

The book opens with a chapter by Dr. Adele Hofmann, a pediatrician who has for several years made adolescent medicine her exclusive interest. Her contribution both states the problem as the non-psychiatrist experiences it and sets the tone for what is to follow. There follow chapters each devoted to a specific area of adolescent life such as sexuality, drug use, depression and psychosomatic problems. The final chapter serves as counterpoint to the opener and is the psychiatrist's statement of the over-all issue, as well as an attempt to pull the whole together.

Throughout, emphasis has been placed on a simple, concise, and straight-forward presentation avoiding esoteric terminology and explaining more complex concepts. The family physician in his usual context has everywhere been the reference point and practical, useful information the goal. The result is a small handbook for working with adolescents that should find its place on the busy doctor's bookshelf, yet get much use.

CONTENTS

The Emotionally
Troubled Adolescent
and the
Family Physician

CHAPTER 1

ADOLESCENT MEDICINE
AND THE TROUBLED YOUTH
AN OVERVIEW

ADELE D. HOFMANN, M.D.

T HE PHYSICIAN IN general practice, pediatrics or internal medicine who provides care to teenagers may well find himself taxed in meeting his youthful patient's emotional needs which arise either in relation to organic concerns or as a primary cause of the problem at hand. As an overview to the more detailed discussions of emotional disturbances elsewhere in this book, this chapter seeks to present a brief history of adolescent medicine and to discuss some of the special health needs and modalities of rendering care to this age group. Within this framework, emotional conflicts are explored and some suggestions as to how the extent of this conflict may be assessed and therapeutic decisions reached and implemented are offered.

The History of Adolescent Medicine

Adolescent medicine, progressing through its own crisis for identity and independence, has only recently reached its majority. The first program of record devoted exclusively to serving adolescents and to teaching the care of this age group to physicians was initiated at the Boston Children's Hospital in 1951 by Dr. Roswell Gallagher. As physician to the Hill School in Pennsylvania he had become acutely aware of the often neglected health problems of teen-aged youth and the special techniques required to provide them with optimal care. Prior to this time medicine generally regarded adolescents as big children or small adults with little attention to the unique aspects of their physical and emotional development. The Boston unit sought to fill this gap and in the ensuing 20 years or so has been followed by many more units, the "Free Youth Clinic" movement and more recently by increasing numbers of private practitioners coming to care for teen-agers in what might be termed an *age-oriented* approach.

Certainly adolescent medicine was an idea whose time had come. Physicians in the late 1940's and early 1950's, having been provided with infinitely more effective methods for combating organic disease, found time to consider the behavioral as well as biological aspects of patient care. The number of adolescents in the world was rapidly increasing. In the United States alone the 21 million 10 to 19 year olds identified in the 1950 census would increase nearly twofold to 39 million by 1970. And lastly, the concept of age oriented medical attention to adolescents would see its confirmation and societal acceptance, if not demand, in the health problems engendered by the rapid changes in youth life-styles of the mid-sixty's with its increasing venereal disease rates, rising numbers of out-of-wedlock births, drug abuse epidemics and increased acute illness among run-away youngsters inhabiting crash pads or urban communes. Perhaps we will soon see a new dimension and demand as large numbers of handicapped infants who previously failed to survive are now salvaged and come into their teen years.

In a 1962 poll, special services for adolescents existed in 24 of some 300 hospitals in the United States and Canada, only two of which had been established before 1955. Just nine years later this number had increased to at least 73 with an additional 14 planning similar efforts in the near future. Fellowship programs have risen from Boston's lone unit in 1952 to 29 in 1971 accommodating 46 candidates with 24 additional programs potentially available within the next five years. The vast preponderance of these programs are in University affiliated hospitals. One thus sees a direction wherein it can be anticipated that attention to the health needs of adolescents will shortly become a part of the curriculum of most medical schools and a responsibility of all physicians.

Health Needs of Adolescents

One might well ask at this point, what is adolescent medicine? Indeed the second decade are years when mortality and serious morbidity are low as compared to other times in life. Our mind's eye, perhaps enviously, envisages teen-agers as possessing buoyant good health, singularly resistant to illness and the ravages of passing years or the frailties of infancy. Yet substantial medical needs do exist. Rogers and Reese found a 40 percent incidence of medical defects among white middle class high school students. Surveys among inner city youths have found up to 60 percent have untreated remediable conditions. Adolescent clinics quickly fill their appointment books well in advance with youths and their parents seeking assistance for a wide variety of problems; psychosomatic disorders, behavioral problems, allergies, respiratory tract disease, obesity and menstrual irregularities often leading the list.

Today we must surely include venereal disease, pregnancy, drug abuse and related problems high on the list of reasons for which youngsters need medical attention. The recent recognition that youths afflicted with these problems must be able to consent to confidential care on their own and the concomitant spectacular increase in enabling laws in nearly every state now permit many youths suffering from these sensitive problems to obtain the treatment they were heretofore reluctant to seek when parental consent was a prerequisite. Indeed, these problems may well represent the area of greatest health need for today's adolescent. It has been estimated that one teen-ager in the United States becomes infected with venereal disease every 75 seconds and that at least two out of every hundred school girls will become pregnant in any given year. Drug abuse exists in every community and economic class and there is little evidence that it will abate in the near future.

There are relatively few organic conditions which are largely limited to the second decade. Except for pubertal developmental problems, certain orthopedic abnormalities, acne and a few other relatively rare conditions the majority of health problems are those seen in other years as well, bridging the spectrum of diseases of children and adults. But in adolescence, as at perhaps no other time in life, there is an intense interplay between the psychodynamic impact and organic pathology of any disease situation. Youths can neither resort to the passive dependence of the young child nor the insightful acceptance of the adult, but must wrestle with coping on their own terms at some point in between.

Adolescents are rapidly growing in stature to where they no longer feel dwarfed by surrounding adults, literally able to look them straight in the eye for the first time and biologically capable of reproducing their own species. Emotionally they are emancipating themselves, finding their identity, determining their moral value codes and deciding on future careers. Capable of considerable independence they still need adult support, trust and encouragement within a setting of firm but gradually expanding limits despite their frequent and vigorous protests and testing to the contrary. They need to be able to touch base at home, to find a place where they are loved and accepted yet spend increasingly longer times away from family and within the peer group discovering who they are and trying out various roles held up to the mirror of their friends' acceptance or rejection. At no other time in life, excepting the first twelve months, are there more rapid, profound and unique emotional and physical changes.

It is within this framework that adolescent medicine functions, seeing the youth as an individual with responses to illness or medical needs substantially different from that of other decades. The handicapped youth will be more acutely distressed by his inability to physically master and control his environment than at any other age. A chronically ill adolescent must come to grips with the implication of his condition in relation to his hopes for a career, marriage and family. A girl with a disfiguring condition may be so discomforted by her cognitive perception of unattractiveness as to withdraw and become seriously depressed. A youth with previously well managed diabetes may become difficult to control out of his denial of his deficiency or, alternatively, out of using it to manipulate and threaten his parents for secondary gain. A youngster placed on forced bed rest may panic at the loss of his newly found independence and disruptively act out or become depressed and withdrawn.

On the other side of the coin, it is extremely common in

adolescent years to find emotional stress and anxiety displaced onto bodily symptomatology. At no other time are we so narcissistically preoccupied with physical development, often carefully inspecting each minute progression toward maturity with a mixture of intense delight and acute embarassment. One cannot separate biological from emotional change and the singular anxiety that arises out of adolescent emotional conflicts, normal or abnormal, may not always be resolvable or manageable at the psychic level, bubbling over into physical symptomatology.

Preventive medicine for the adolescent also has this dual psychophysiological mix approach and will largely concern itself with youngsters who act out with behavior which involves substantial medical risk as in preventing venereal disease, unwanted babies, drug addiction and its medical complications or the increase in acute illnesses often experienced by the run-away living under hygienically and nutritionally compromised circumstances. Perhaps an even greater preventive challenge presents itself in understanding the psychodynamics which underlie adolescent accidents and injuries, the number one cause of death and disability in this age group.

An Approach to the Adolescent Patient

At all points then, adolescent medicine is concerned with meeting not only medical needs but also taking into account emotional aspects, social or environmental factors and the patient's particular level of maturation at the given moment in time.

Thus the medical care of the adolescent includes:

1. The diagnosis and treatment of the presenting problem.
2. The discovery of heretofore unmet medical needs whether they be acne, dental caries, vision and hearing defects or gonorrhea.
3. The provision of preventive health measures from tuberculin skin testing and updating immunizations to counselling and education on sexuality, drug abuse, smoking and the like and preventive services including contraception when indicated.
4. Identification and rectification, through direct intervention or referral, of emotional and social problems related or unrelated to the presenting complaint.
5. Counselling and attention to the fulfillment of the patient's career and life-style goals, particularly if the medical condition may interfere.

6. The use of the physician and other health care personnel as a maturational force and role models. For many youths relationships with concerned and sensitive members of the medical team may well provide him with a meaningful experience of aid in his search for identity and sense of self-worth.

7. Assisting the patient to develop and institute sound views and practices of preventive and restitutive health care and health knowledge for his adult life and future family.

This may sound like a monumental task for the busy practitioner. It cannot be denied that the adolescent patient does require more time than others. But it need not be unwieldy or impossible and an extra 10 minutes well used will often pay off. First the stage needs be set. The adolescent is ready, willing and able to talk about his own problems and is generally an excellent historian. The majority of the recent history should be obtained from the patient directly and in private with the adolescent, not the parent, the focus in communications. The time when the physician and parents talked about the child as if he were some inanimate object has passed. Of course the parent has a vested interest and needs to know diagnostic and therapeutic plans as well as having much historical information unavailable to the patient. An interview with the mother or father can be held either several days before or during the initial patient visit. If done during the initial visit, this should be held in the presence of the patient unless the particular circumstances warrant otherwise. Even when a separate parent-doctor interview is held it is generally wise to tell the adolescent the gist of what was discussed lest he come to see the physician as an ally of the *over 35 generation* rather than as being on his side.

The patient should understand that he and not the parent is expected to be responsible for following recommendations and keeping appointments. He should also be encouraged to come by himself if he wishes and parents will allow. Confidences are to be respected and the youth so advised. In the event that privileged information is uncovered that absolutely requires parental involvement, it is generally not difficult to help the adolescent see the necessity and agree to this.

In the conduct of the interview itself it is helpful to obtain information about why medical care is being sought from both the parent and the youth, as well as the school or outside agency if they have instigated the visit. Often all will have different perceptions as to the need. The patient, particularly, may often see him or herself as having no problem or a quite different one from others and may be resentful at being forced to come. It should also be kept in mind that the presenting complaint may well be just a screen for, or symptomatic of, a more difficult or more sensitive need. It is not unusual for an adolescent girl to come with headaches only to discover under confidential circumstances that she fears she is pregnant, that a boy with concern for a slow puberty is really worried about homosexual impulses or that a teen-ager who is tired all the time doesn't have the mononucleosis his family suspects but instead has a school problem.

In addition to the usual past history and family history it is also helpful to ask about adolescent habits and social behavioral patterns. Young people usually respond positively to this evidence of interest in them as whole individuals by the physician and, although perhaps startled, rarely resent it. Information covering diet, exercise, sleep, smoking, alcohol and drugs should provide some clues as to the life style of the patient and offer information as to what specific areas may require health education or other therapeutic measures. While this is a natural and logical time to ask about drug abuse, it should be kept in mind that patient information on drugs, or for that matter on any other sensitive topic, obtained in the initial interview before trust has been won, is often something less than the true state of affairs. Care should be exercised not to force a possible false negative commitment which the patient may then find difficult to reverse in the future.

In regards to social history, interviewing should provide an assessment of the present level of maturity, psycho-social functioning and future goals. Evaluation of relationships within family, school and peers, the three worlds of the adolescent, should serve to determine whether social and emotional development is progressing without major problems or not. Sometimes the youth needs to be encouraged to give his views. Often reluctant to reveal family conflicts to strangers, he may need to be reassured that it is normal for there to be some disagreements between parents and adolescent and asked if he, like many others, has problems about curfew hours, allowance, where he or she may go or what can be worn. The reluctant youth may be further helped to verbalize his concerns by applying the *three wishes* concept and determining what three things he would like to see changed at home. Another technique is in having the patient rate his home compared to those of his friends as better, about the same or worse.

School evaluation allows assessment of intellectual capacity and utilization, of the appropriateness of career and vocational goals and serves to identify school problems and the actual or potential drop-out. Questioning generally presents little problem and covers how they like school, how they are doing, what are their future plans, whether they have curricular tracking problems and if school difficulties exist what steps are being taken to correct them.

As the formation of peer relationships among members of both the same and opposite sex is a vital part of adolescence, whether the patient has close friends with whom they share everything and is dating or not gives further evidence as to maturational progress. Dating behavior, of course, must be appropriate to the patient's age and economic or cultural factors. Some girls may not be allowed to go out with boys until an age well past their desire to do so and even may not be allowed away from home other than during school hours. Other youths may well have social activities curtailed by an after school or weekend job. Talking about dating patterns also affords a setting for determining the need for sex counselling, education and possible therapy including contraception. Most adolescents will not initiate a discussion on sexual matters, but all are intensely concerned and often welcome the opportunity. In identifying sexually active teenagers the appropriateness of questions to where the youth is *at* cannot be stressed enough. One need not go further with a girl who has never dated or only casually done so and only in groups. But one who is going steady and spends long periods of time alone with someone she thinks she might like to marry is another matter and should be directly asked as to whether they have sexual intercourse together or not.

While there generally is no difficulty in questioning about behavior itself, caution needs be exercised as to how deeply intimate fears and concerns should be probed. Development of mutual trust and confidence and proper timing of questions is of the essence. Such queries will generally be fruitless and may even be harmful in raising emotional issues that the adolescent is not yet ready to handle if pushed too vigorously too soon. For the youth who doesn't wish to talk about a particular problem it is often best simply to open the door and give the patient the option of either picking up the topic at that moment or reopening it at some later visit.

Perhaps the most important ingredient of the adolescent visit is the attitude and approach of the physician himself. The youth, hopefully, will come to view his doctor as an empathetic and understanding friend and as someone to be trusted and confided in. The physician is on the side of the patient, but does not side with maladaptive behavior. He is his patient's advocate. He understands the nature of adolescent growth and development and the inherent problems of parent-child conflicts, yet avoiding the pitfall of becoming a parent surrogate or imposing his own values and morals. He listens to the youth without judging, setting up a dialogue whereby the patient is helped to explore his own feelings, beliefs and values. He recognizes the intense concern adolescents have for their developing bodies and takes even relatively minor concerns seriously, offering reassurance and support. When indicated he provides straightforward medical and biological facts, keeping in mind that adolescent misinformation is monumental despite most school health and sex education programs. When the adolescent is ill or needs surgery he takes time to explain what is going on, what will happen, what he is going to do and why and affords frequent opportunity for the youth to ask questions.

The physician who follows these guidelines will find many rewards in being of significant help to the adolescent. His is a unique role. The youth, often at odds with his family as he realigns his relationship to them from childish dependancy to adult friendship, often has no other adult figure in his life in whom he can openly confide. Teachers are often preoccupied with the group educational process. Ministers, priests and rabbis have a theological dogma to uphold. Police are bound to implement the law and are generally held in poor regard by young people. The physician need be none of these and may relate to the adolescent, unencumbered, as a meaningful extra-parental adult and role model whose advice and council may frequently be sought for emotional as well as physical needs.

Assessing the Emotionally Troubled Youth

Within this framework the emotionally disturbed adolescent may present under a number of guises. Most clearly there is the parent who brings the youth with a complaint highly suggestive of an emotional disorder such as school failure, disruptive behavior or suicidal attempt. But one must also be alert to this possibility when faced with psychosomatic complaints, a youth with hepatitis, a girl who asks for contraception or simply in the course of a routine medical contact. In a recent survey of youths presenting with medical complaints, 46 percent were found to also have some form of emotional or social maladaptation requiring intervention beyond just meeting biological needs. Of these, 31 percent were caused by or causative of the presenting complaint, but 15 percent were not so related and were only uncovered by a comprehensive history.

Those situations in which the physician will particularly need to assess emotional integrity generally fall into four different categories. In the order most frequently seen in the physician's office, first is the youth with physical symptoms secondary to emotional stress. Second is the adolescent engaging in certain secretive risky activities usually at odds with parental wishes. Thirdly there is the patient who is brought for clear cut emotional or behavioral problems often related to deteriorating school performance or loss of parental control. And lastly is the youngster who comes for relatively simple and clear cut medical need either as a purposeful screen to provide the opportunity to talk about something else more sensitive or troubling or when unrecognized or unadmitted emotional problems are otherwise brought to light.

It is a common experience in the office for a youngster to come with complaints for which no organic cause can be found. The close and inseparable interplay between physical and emotional development of adolescents has already been alluded to. Headaches, stomach aches, dizzy spells, easy fatiguability, assorted muscle pains and feeling tired all the time are frequent symptoms. The patient with psychogenic origins of these complaints will often suffer from more than one, or even all in what may be termed the *multiple complaint syndrome* and one's suspicion for underlying causal emotional stress rises with the addition of each new organ system to the list of problems. In addition one may look for vagueness in the nature of the pain or discomfort. Headaches or stomach aches may occur at any time of the day, are difficult to describe and are only variably relieved by symptomatic medication or rest. On the other hand complaints secondary to organic disease are usually much more circumscribed, often can be well defined by the patient and frequently occur under reproducible and predictable circumstances. Of course a diagnosis of psychosomatic or hysterical illness must always be one of exclusion and even when the physician's initial differential considerations places this high on the list a full medical evaluation is always indicated. Liver function tests, a heterophile or a sedimentation rate and the like will be positive just often enough to caution against jumping to conclusions.

Once organic disease has been eliminated as a possibility, the next step is in determining whether the underlying emotional cause is simply a result of normal adolescent conflicts, related to a reality based environmental situation or is truely indicative of serious emotional disturbance. In the first instance adolescents in the midst of their emancipation struggle or pubertal development may experience any number of vague aches and pains. However, many youths so afflicted will be found to be progressing reasonably well at home, school and among peers. Simple support and reassurance with periodic revisits often is all that is necessary. In the second instance an adolescent may react with bodily symptoms in the face of important examinations, curricular difficulties and school record mix-ups, the break-up of an important friendship, the loss of a loved family member etc. Intervention needs be practical and oriented toward solving the problem or ventilating grief. With a serious psychiatric problem other evidences of poor emotional functioning will be forthcoming from the history and a consideration of possible referral for psychiatric treatment may well be entertained.

The next most commonly encountered situation might be called *the scruff of the neck syndrome.* An adolescent is almost literally dragged into the physician's office with his or her mother highly upset and accusatory, demanding that the doctor prove their youngster is using drugs or is being sexually promiscuous, often thrusting forward a mangled cigarette, unidentified capsule or contraceptives found in the child's clothing or room. It often takes heroic efforts on the part of the physician not to succumb to being a policeman. Quiet interviews with parent and child separately will help to begin to sift fact from fantasy. Perhaps there are no deeper seated fears among many parents today than that their adolescent might be engaging in drug abuse or sexual activity. But here again the situation cannot be resolved unless the confidence and trust of the youth is won. It does little good to prove that drugs exist in the urine or that the hymen is not intact if the patient is so alienated by the process that communications break down on all fronts. A corollary situation is the youth who comes requesting contraception or fearing pregnancy or with medical complications of drug abuse such as serum hepatitis and skin abscesses or where these secretive behavior patterns are uncovered as a part of the routine history and examination.

In each instance the totality of the meaning of uncovered drug usage or sexual activity must be explored. Are the behavior patterns simply experimental and derived out of cultural peer pressures and expectations in an essentially normal youth or are they symptomatic of more serious psychopathology providing surcease for unresolvable emotional conflicts or resulting in a self-destructive, exploitative alternative to more effective adaptational mechanisms?

When significant psychopathology is uncovered the physician will again come to consider referring the youth for therapy. But if the adolescent appears to be relatively intact, intervention is geared toward exploring the youth's feelings about his behavior, providing him with solid medical facts, assisting him to make his own decisions after being provided with a clear picture of consequences and alternatives and perhaps most importantly helping him to learn how to say "no" under peer pressure. There can be no alternative to "no" for drug abuse. However, the physician may be confronted with a different situation with the sexually active teen-age girl who has lost any value that might accrue to her from virginity, feels little guilt and sees nothing wrong in having sexual intercourse. Certainly there are good arguments that sexual relationships require a maturity not possessed by the young adolescent for their optimal emotional meaning and may well result in psychic trauma and thus should be avoided. But studies by the Presidential Commission on Population Control and the American Future have found that some 47 percent of teen-aged girls have had sexual intercourse by the age of 19 years, suggesting that valid cultural and moral patterns are emerging that did not exist in the time of our victorian forefathers. Thus caution is required in evaluating whether continuing sexual activity per se in adolescence is related to significant emotional disorder or not. In any event therapy should also include protection against the serious consequences of sexual intercourse in a teen-ager by contraception and venereal disease counselling.

The problems encountered in assessing the youth brought with ostensibly clear-cut emotional needs may not always be as obvious as they first appear. A youth with borderline mental retardation may have been able to adequately succeed in school until his secondary years when frustration at no longer being able to keep up may manifest itself in acting out behavior or withdrawal. The youngster who is brought in because the parents can no longer control him may only be expressing relatively normal strivings for independence and it is rather the parent who is upset and threatened by these intimations of their child's emancipation. A girl whose mother brings her for a school problem and because she seems withdrawn may have missed her last two menstrual periods and believe herself to be pregnant. These and similar situations suggest alertness to the fact that things are not always exactly what they seem to be on the surface, and a careful history is always indicated to separate the youth who is truly emotionally disturbed from the one who is reactively upset in response to a valid reality situation.

Any of the above problems may also exist in a youth who comes for some other purpose. In particular, the screen complaint should be looked for. One should be alert to such a situation when, for instance, an adolescent comes for an examination at a time when such is not needed for school, camp or job. It is doubtful that many adolescents will voluntarily seek just an annual physical when it is not required. Others may have fabricated vague aches and pains to provide the opportunity to talk with someone confidentially about an emotional or sensitive matter. And lastly, emotional disturbances, often of a serious nature, may well exist untreated but the patient and parents do not consider it within the purview of the visit when, say, the youth may need care for some organic disorder or required exam. While it is inappropriate to discuss detailed family or school problems with an acutely ill or injured youth, some identifying enquiries are routinely in order when he returns for a later check and is feeling better or for the youth who is not in acute discomfort at any time. While the adolescent is being examined the physician may simply and naturally ask how things are going at school, at home and among his friends. Occasionally a major disturbance may unexpectedly come to light.

Managing the Emotional Conflict

Once the physician has determined that an emotional conflict indeed exists, he must first define whether this is due to a significant emotional disorder or whether the problem is simply a result of normal adolescent stresses. Then a decision needs to be made on what therapeutic course to pursue; whether his own support and guidance will be sufficient or whether psychiatric referral is indicated. In either case the next step is the development of a relationship of trust and confidence. If he continues to treat the patient such a relationship is fundamental. If a referral is planned such will be of assistance in motivating the youth to accept it. Obviously a psychiatrist will have a difficult time with a reluctant youth determined not to cooperate, perceiving the problem to rest with other people and with no awareness of his own contributions to the conflict.

Certainly the youth with conflicts and concerns within the scope of normal adolescence will usually respond well to short term support by the doctor himself. Some of these situations have already been reviewed. With more serious problems a number of points may help to recommend one therapeutic approach over the other and largely depend on the degree, duration and manifestations of the disturbance as well as the willingness of the youth and his parents to entertain a psychiatric diagnosis and accept a psychiatric referral.

Other chapters in this book will describe particular situations in detail, but in general the following points may be found helpful in assessing the seriousness of the disorder. First from the parents, in this instance best interviewed alone, what kind of a child has the patient been? Has he been thought to be doing well until recently or has he always been seen as a difficult child? How has he performed in school? Has he achieved reasonably well or has he always had problems? Has he had close friends or has he more or less been a loner and preferred to be by himself? Lastly do the parents see the difficulty as a serious long term emotional problem now come to a crisis, as a serious problem but of recent onset, as a loss of their ability to control the youth or in some other light? During this interview the physician will also be assessing the emotional integrity of the parents. Are they realistic in their expectations for their child? Are they appropriately encouraging him to be independent but with realistic limits that they usually succeed in imposing or are they either overprotective, continuing to infantilize the youth on the one hand or overpermissive having abdicated from efforts to control excesses on the other? Are the home and parental interrelationships such that there has been a stable nurturing environment or have there been disruptions such as quarrels, alcoholism, prolonged parental absence, divorce etc.?

In the interview with youth himself perhaps the most important aspect will be the impression of the youth's affect as he tells his side of the conflict provided he views the physician as his ally and not that of the parents. Is the youngster capable of a positive relationship? Are there evidences of warmth and humor and some degree of insight, or is he only withdrawn, depressed or angry? Further, what does the youth feel the problem is and does he realistically perceive himself as contributing to the situation to some degree or does he feel that his troubles are solely the result of lack of understanding by the outside world? In terms of his life-style, does he have friends and, if age-appropriate, date? How does he see himself in relation to his parents and school? Does he have realistic plans for the next five years or so?

A further and often enlightening point will be to observe what happens when parents and youth are interviewed together. Does the youngster comfortably look to the parents for support in working things out and are the parents responsive or do they enter into a mutually antagonistic and alienating situation? After conducting these three interviews an idea as to the seriousness of the disturbance should emerge. At all points the underlying question to be asked is whether this particular youth is headed for personal self-fulfillment in some form of a reasonably responsible life-style, even if at some variance with parental or the physician's own value systems, or not. Such fulfillment rests upon the ability of the individual to view himself with esteem as a person of worth and to make meaningful relationships with others.

With youths in a reactive situation of relatively recent onset the therapeutic mode largely rests with the physician. To see them for 30 to 40 minutes every week or two for several months may be most beneficial. The purpose of such sessions is essentially to help the youth ventilate his feelings, understand how his actions interfere with more constructive directions, come to more effectively interact with those around him, make reasoned rather than impulsive decisions and ultimately come to a better sense of self esteem.

The course of a visit, then, may well begin by reviewing recent events and empathically exploring the latest conflicts at school or home, allowing the patient to express his indignation, anger or disappointment. Successful and positive experiences can also be examined to keep a balanced perspective. This is followed by a shared exploration of the effectiveness of the youth's responses; did he gain very much by *blowing his stack* or by staying out later than he was supposed to or conversely what ingredients went into making up the peaceful, non-confrontational weekend at home. The last stage is exploring alternative solutions to conflictual situations, strengthening the more effective alternatives even by role playing or rehearsal and reinforcing the positive aspects of the patient's personality and his concept of self worth.

The physician will also need to confer with parents or school to help them and the youth together set realistic limits and the penalties for their violation but without entering into unconstructive power struggles. The use of community resources such as athletic programs, local youth centers, ecology projects, craft centers, part time jobs and the like may also be helpful situations where the adolescents can actively participate in positive decisions, actions and accomplishments which will be well regarded by both peers and adults or where he can earn an income of his own. Such may well provide him with the successes he needs to counter the reactive situation which, in adolescence, often results out of inner perceptions of failure and inadequacy.

Adolescents with deep seated disturbances of long duration or whose symptomatology presents significant danger to himself or others or where supportive treatment of a less disturbed youngster has failed will warrant referral. Problems may exist in motivating the youth to accept this. Many are often leary of psychiatrists, understanding little of the therapeutic process. They may feel that to enter into psychiatric treatment will label them as being *crazy*. There is a fear about the unknown. What will happen; what is it like; will I lose control; will I reveal more that I want to; will my secrets be discovered in spite of myself? It is not unusual to find that teen-agers believe psychiatrists have powers which enable them to read minds. In preparing the youth, then, he needs to be reassured that he is not *crazy* but rather that he has taken a detour in his maturational progress and needs the assistance of a trained professional to help him get back on the right track. He needs to have his fears allayed and be reassured that the psychiatrist has no magical tools, but does know young people and will, through talking, simply help him to look into himself and come to know his own strengths and weaknesses and to manage them more effectively than he has in the past. One may further capitalize on the youth's normal narcissism and invite his enjoyment of a situation where he has the undivided attention of a non-judgmental adult on a regular basis.

At times one finds some patients, particularly those with acting-out types of behavior problems, who are totally unable to accept such a referral or whose parents refuse to accept a psychiatric diagnosis. The practitioner may well have to carry such adolescents on his own for a time. Such young people can often make good relationships with the physician whom they or their parents feel to be less threatening. Carrying out the supportive program outlined for the less disturbed reactive adolescent may be helpful in at least averting further deterioration and again consists of verbalization of the patient's concerns and relatively concrete reality-based management of day to day functioning. With time, as the patient comes to be able to open up to the physician he may then be able to accept transfer to a psychiatrist. When the parents are the blocking force, similar approaches can be taken with them. However, the outcome is less apt to be felicitous as parental incapacity which is so disabling as to render them unable to accept emotional disturbance in their child must result out of a fairly profound and long standing fixed disability within themselves.

Of course some youths may refuse referral but are so disturbed that practical supportive measures alone are inadequate and even may be dangerous. Suicidal adolescents, those with a chronic history of exceedingly poor impulse control or those on the brink of a psychotic break are some examples. Under these conditions the physician and parents must promptly take over regardless of the youth's verbalized resistance. It can be assumed that such youngsters are deeply frightened by their overwhelming inner impulses and will really welcome firm controls and having protective action taken on their behalf.

Thus the physician who cares for adolescents will find himself best able to meet the needs of this age group when an approach is adopted which at all points meets both his patient's physical and emotional needs in equal and balanced measure. The methods outlined herein offer a framework in which this approach may be implemented. In relation to emotional problems the doctor will offer support and guidance to some and for others he will recognize the disturbance as beyond his capacity, preparing and motivating the youth and parents for referral and following through with continued back-up and support of this course.

BIBLIOGRAPHY

1. Daniel, W.A.: *The Adolescent Patient*. St. Louis, Mosby, 1970.
2. Gallagher, J.R.: *Medical Care of the Adolescent*. 2nd Ed. New York, Appleton-Century-Crofts, 1966.
3. Hammer, S.L. and Holterman, V.: Interviewing and counseling adolescent patients. *Clin Pediatr, 9:*47-53, 1970.
4. Health Problems of Adolescence, Technical Report Series # 308. World Health Organization. New York Columbia University Press, International Documents Service.
5. Kappelman, M.M.: The adolescent and his dangers. *Clin Pediatr, 10:*154-159, 1971.
6. Schonfeld, W.A.: Body-image in adolescence; a psychiatric concept for the pediatrician. *Pediatrics, 31:*845-855, 1963.
7. Stephenson, J.R.: Communication in adolescent medicine. *Clin Pediatr, 9:*558-564, 1970.
8. Weinberg, S.: Suicidal intent in adolescence: a hypothesis about the role of physical illness. *J Pediatr, 77:*579-586, 1970.
9. Winnicott, D.W.: Adolescent process and the need for personal confrontation. *Pediatrics, 44:*752-756, 1969.

CHAPTER 2

THE PRESENT DAY ADOLESCENT —
HEALTHY AND NEUROTIC

MARTIN SYMONDS, M.D.

IT IS COMMONALLY ACCEPTED that the child, as he becomes older, will undergo physiological changes and become an adolescent. Merely getting older, however, does not insure normal emotional development. In childhood, where satisfaction of dependency needs is primary and required for physical survival, emotional development is directly related to the sense of security provided the child. If, in these earlier years, too much effort has gone into insuring his own survival, there will be serious interference with the second phase of emotional maturation which has been called *the who am I* phase, the phase of self realization or the development of the sense of identity. This second phase can be called psychological adolescence. If dependency needs are adequately satisfied in childhood, this second phase of personality development will take place during the adolescent years. If not, the second phase will be delayed and sometimes never develop.

There are people who seem to have gone from childhood to adulthood without experiencing psychological adolescence. Some of these individuals, when they are in their thirties or even late forties, become aware of an inner restlessness. They talk about their need to find themselves. They have become tired of being yes men or robots. They search for a lost self through romance and adventure. They become daring in their choice of clothing and even hair styles. They appear to be going through a delayed psychological adolescence.

This concept of psychological adolescence is of clinical importance. It helps us understand some of the confusion and the communication gaps that exist between parents and youngsters. Parents who for varying reasons have gone from childhood to adulthood and sidestepped their adolescence view almost every aspect of adolescent behavior with alarm and call it sick. In addition, all adults seem to have a degree of amnesia for their adolescent years. In courses on adolescence that I have taught to either parents or professional workers, I have often asked who would be willing to re-live his adolescent years and found that 90 percent of the class would not want to. Adolescence is not often remembered as a happy time in one's life. Of course, this may be the result of retrospective distortion rather than a reflection of how that individual's adolescence was actually spent. However, the exploration and experimentation necessary for healthy emotional growth involves much turbulence and many painful experiences. For example, in developing his autonomy from parental control, the adolescent must separate and differentiate his goals from parental expectations. If his parents equate their youngster's attempts to grow away from them as acts against them, they will resist his moves, creating great stress for the boy. Example:

John is a 17 year old, high school graduate who decides to take a year or more off from school in order to work as an actor. He would like the same financial support his parents promised him if he went to college. John's father now refuses to talk to him since he feels John has embarrassed him before his friends. He feels he has been made to look foolish, since he had made all kinds of contacts to get John into his own alma mater. John's mother is upset, since she is ashamed to tell her friends what John plans to do. Even John's sister is angry with him. She feels his proposed desire to become an actor may imperil her impending marriage with a clergyman.

Society rarely encourages the adolescent to self-discovery, experimentation and exploration. Parental guidance usually reinforces society's values and is frequently homiletic, filled with stories of "how, when a child didn't listen to his parents, he was lost." Familiar themes of parental advice are:

Listen to the teacher, he knows best. Smoking stunts your

growth. A person is known by the company he keeps (an urban variant of this theme is "Stay away from those bums"). As to sex, the advice runs the gamut from, "Don't think about it," to "exercise and study hard." Even playing the piano has been used to exorcise sexual desire.

In his response to all this, the youngster may accentuate the communication gap, as he becomes pre-occupied with disguising the smell of *grass* or whether a pimple might be a syphilitic chancre. It is characteristic of the adolescent to be morbidly and narcissistically pre-occupied and self-absorbed. This trait frequently leads to agonizing reappraisals of all psychological solutions of childhood. This re-examination most often focusses on conformity, which is a successful solution of childhood. It comes to be seen by the adolescent as the compliancy of *just being a robot* and as such becomes a despised way of life, only for *squares* or *creeps*. The youngster intends to cleanse or purge himself of all vestiges of compliancy. He does not distinguish between compliancy and conformity. He lumps all "yes" behavior to authority as compliancy and despises it. However, the distinction between compliancy and conformity must be maintained for healthy emotional growth. Conformity is an integral part of the process of developing group identity; compliancy is necessary behavior to preserve group belonging.

Conforming is behaving in ways approved of by the establishment. The conforming individual has successfully incorporated these standards, seeing these values as his own. Compliancy is also behavior approved by the establishment, which, however, the individual experiences as submission to authority out of fear, feeling that to act otherwise would lead to group disapproval and ostracism. To the observer, compliant and conforming behavior may seem identical but the subject is aware of the difference. For example: A man may wear the emblem of the American flag in his lapel because he is proud to be an American and show it (conforming behavior). Another may wear the emblem in his lapel because he is afraid of being thought of as a "Commie" (compliant behavior). In healthy emotional development both conforming and compliant behavior are necessary components. It is only when such behavior takes on a compulsive quality that it can be called neurotic.

In his attempts to purify himself the adolescent develops what I have called the *wet paint* syndrome. When a child sees a sign *wet paint* on a bench, he doesn't touch the bench either out of fear or respect. The adult obeys it, in addition, from experience. It is in the nature of the adolescent, when he sees such a sign, to touch the bench with his hand, look at the paint on his fingers, wipe them off on his trousers and say, "Yes, it is wet paint." The *wet paint* syndrome has been frequently misinterpreted as a lack of respect for authority, defiance, stupidity and even viewed as paranoid, but it is the adolescent's way of discovering the real world. He can no longer blindly accept another's statement or interpretation of reality. He does this in many areas of his life to the frustration and despair of his parents who want to spare him the expense and sometimes the grief of trying out everything for himself.

As I reviewed the past 15 years in which I have been involved with adolescents and their problems, I developed certain criteria for evaluating adolescent behavior. These criteria have helped me to distinguish behavior the youngster could be expected to outgrow from behavior that is likely to continue and result in an emotionally crippled adult. One indicator I use is the energy level of the adolescent. It has been my experience that adolescents with high energy fare better than those with low energy. Low energy or apathy is a poor clinical sign for healthy emotional growth and is an equivalent of depression. It also indicates the behavior of a passive resistant personality, who always feels and despises his passivity while everyone else experiences his reluctance, resentment or resistance. Energy to me comprises interest, involvement and growth. It should not be confused with mere movement or activity. For example: A boy tells me he likes automobiles. When I explore this interest with him and find the sum total of his involvement in cars is to drive a fast, flashy and expensive car and that he is not at all interested in what is under the hood, I call this pseudo-energy and consider it a poor clinical sign. On the other hand, if he speaks of fuel injection systems, piston displacement ratios and all kinds of esoteric information about Cougars, Jaguars and Mustangs, I am more optimistic about his prospects for growing up as a healthy adult.

The use of energy as here defined is intimately related to the adolescent's need to be a unique person, distinct from his family. In his pursuit of autonomy, the young person may feel he can differ from his parents only by *acting* differently. In trying to understand such behavior, I have found it useful to differentiate oppositional and rebellious behavior.[1] I have defined rebellion as the healthy aspect of adolescent protest in which the young person differs with authority but retains a sense of self. It is quite different from oppositional behavior, a form of adolescent protest in which the individual says "no" or acts "no" before the question is expressed. There is no concern for his own best interests and as such oppositional behavior is neurotic. It is compulsive, automatic, and usually provokes the authority to punish rather than discipline. Rebellious behavior is usually a protest in which the young person considers his best interests. It still carries with it respect for authority. This form of behavior requires that the adult listen seriously to what is being expressed and then make a decision that takes into account the interests of both parties.

A basic problem that confronts the present day adolescent is that adults themselves have often lost confidence and hope, and openly express their confusion and anxiety. This creates significant distress in the adolescent who still needs parental guidance. He must then take over and disregard the adult completely. If the captain of an airline were to come into the passenger section and say, "We are lost, I don't know what to do. Does anyone know how to read maps . . . ", it would produce chaos and panic. The captain must contain his anxiety and not share it. One can imagine the effect on patients if doctors openly shared anxieties: "I don't know what to do . . ." It is essential for a physician to contain his anxieties and say nothing to a patient until he is finished deliberating and comes up with a solution or resolution. Yet many parents persist in openly expressing their confusion, their doubts and their anxieties to their children. It has the quality of what I have elsewhere described as *endothermic mothering*[2] in which there is a reversal of roles and the child must comfort and reassure the parent. When adolescents are exposed to this aspect of adult hopelessness, they become frightened and then angry at the adults on whom they have depended. These reactions form the nucleus of adolescent depression.[3] This depression is reflected by apathy and hopelessness. The future loses importance and the adolescent lives only for the present. He may drop out of life through the drug scene and other forms of acting out behavior. Resolution of feelings of depression may be attempted in communal living and political involvement. A 19 year old expressed these thoughts by telling me: "I can wait patiently in line in a cafeteria if I know there will be food enough for me when my turn comes. But if I feel there won't be enough, I'll push and shove to get my share. That's what I feel like when my parents say 'I don't know if there will be a world for you. I'm glad I'm getting older. This world is going to the dogs.' I get furious and sometimes I have to get grass to turn on."

As I look back, I find I am less concerned about certain aspects of adolescent behavior than others. The following is a list of behavior that most adolescents share and might erroneously be thought to be symptomatic of disturbance. I believe that a good deal of it is within the normal range and will be outgrown by most adolescents without psychiatric intervention:

1. Grandiosity.
2. Pseudo-cynicism.
3. Excessive need for privacy; e.g. the need to be alone in the center of the living room.
4. Sensitivity to coercion.
5. Fear of commitment.
6. Feelings of confusion—awkward behavior.
7. Impatience with others.
8. Vulnerability to people's opinions.
9. Insomnia.
10. Intense pride and over-concern with self-esteem in every aspect of life.
11. Mild depression is present in most adolescents at some point and self-hatred is usually resolved.

There are other signs that carry a poor prognosis without professional help. I would include the following:

1. Contempt for authority or the feeling that he can seduce or bribe authority to get whatever he wants.

2. Sadism or contempt for the tender feelings of others. Tenderness and compassion are thought of as evidence of weakness. Brutality may be glorified.
3. Demands, based on excessive earlier deprivation, that everyone make up, give special consideration or pay for sufferings.
4. Severe somatization of anxiety.
5. Severe and compulsive behavior.
6. Apathy, as seen in adolsecents with low energy.

In conclusion, in order that the adolescent successfully complete his apprenticeship to adulthood, it is necessary that adults stand firm in their beliefs and leave a definite place for him as he comes into adulthood. Part of the dramatic, even chaotic behavior of the present day adolsecent is a direct result of the open expressions of hopelessness and despair from adults about the present day world, and the increasing sense of urgency in the adolescents that there will not be a world for them when they get older.

BIBLIOGRAPHY

1. Symonds, M., M.D.: The oppositional adolescent—in science and psychoanalysis. Ed. J. Masserman, Vol. 9, pp. 38-45, Grune and Stratton, 1966.
2. Symonds, M., M.D.: Parents of schizophrenic children. *J Acad Psychoanal,* (In press).
3. Symonds, M., M.D.: The depression in adolescence in science and psychoanalysis. Ed. J. Masserman, Vol. 17, pp. 66-71. Grune and Stratton, 1970.

CHAPTER 3

PSYCHOSOMATIC PROBLEMS IN ADOLESCENCE

JOSEPH D. TEICHER, M.D.

THE CLINICIAN WHO TREATS ADOLESCENTS must understand normal adolescence (GAP, 1968) as well as his individual adolescent patient and his family. He can scarcely escape knowing about the social and cultural changes affecting youth, youth customs and youth health. The presently tolerant attitude about abortions, the widespread use of marijuana and alcohol, the increase of venereal disease are well known to him. The effects of today's rock bands and electronic blaring sounds are becoming visible in hearing losses of up to 45 percent in youths and young adults.

The clinician is in a favored status and his profession invites confidence and confidentiality. An accepting, tolerant yet matter of fact attitude laced with warmth and even a sense of humor helps in establishing rapport. Judgmental and moralistic attitudes do not help. Whenever the intensity of symptoms are far out of proportion to the physical evidence, or the illness is severe like anorexia nervosa or mucous colitis, the clinician must learn to inquire into psychological areas focusing on the adolescent, his peers, his family, his studies. Having been the family physician is of inestimable value in assessing the gravity of a problem. It is wise whenever the physician is in doubt to seek the counsel of a psychiatrist, nor should he hesitate to seek a consultation for his patient if the problem appears to him beyond his scope or time.

Adolescence is marked by physical changes. The male is concerned about his bodily appearance, height, muscles and skin.

The girl is concerned about her figure, breasts, height, skin and hair. In short, there is a marked preoccupation with body and with new sensations and perceptions in this biological thrust into adulthood. The psychological tasks of adolescence require assumption of an adult role, freedom from infantile ties with parents, development of a sense of autonomy, the ability to work and to achieve a heterosexual orientation with the capacity to love. The transition to adulthood is not smooth. Often, unresolved problems from early childhood present themselves once again for solution. The healthier the development of the adolescent, the less likely is he to be unduly stressed and show other than *adjustment reactions*. The more disturbed his development, particularly his early years, the more likely is he to demonstrate psychological or somatic disturbances.

The adolescent reacts to physical defect, disability or limitations of any sort as a great threat to his self image. Acne is common and rarely seen other than in adolescents. They suffer with it, feel humiliated and generally feel shame as if somehow one's secret thoughts are visible. The secrets or secret thoughts have to do with sexuality and masturbation. Severe cases of acne are tormenting blemishes and in many instances home remedies and picking merely aggravate the condition. The healthy youth recognizes acne as a maturational change and lives with it. The troubled adolescent may display a variety of problems such as solitariness, depression, obsessive preoccupation about a visibly blemished face and what it may mean to observers, and a hypochondriacal concern about his physical condition generally. One young man worried about daily bowel movement since he was sure retained feces poisoned the body and showed this in acne. The clinician treating adolescents with acne must be aware that attention to the skin is only skin deep and the feelings about the disorder must be dealt with in a supportive, understanding way that will help him to live through this maturational change—or blemish.

Everyone experiences anxiety but adolescents experience it in a more intense way. They are far more aware of internal sensations such as increased heart rate or fatigue. Some develop a hypochrondriacal preoccupation with their symptoms and it may be so marked as to interfere with athletics, social relationships and studies. All appear to be mildly hypochondriacal and it is usually transitory. One healthy young man worried at various times about his kneecap, his back, his wrist. There is much stress accompanying the increase of sexual impulses and about the necessary task of emancipation that threatens the loss of his dependent attachment to his parents. The adolescent readily responds with the development of physical symptoms. It is important to remember that the various parts of the body have symbolic meanings, i.e. the head, eye, nose, teeth, etc. Symptoms involving any part of the body, thus, have a special meaning and physical illness or damage to any part of the body has its unique psychological importance. "The emotional turbulence of the adolescent, because of the inner pressures it creates, is only too ready to attach itself to any somatic disorder, intensifying its symptomatology to such a degree that the clinician will often be surpised by the intensity of the symptoms with such minor physical changes." (Harris, p. 239).

A variety of psychosomatic disorders have their onset in adolescence. There appears to be little incentive for parents noting active somatic symptoms to seek psychological help, a reality which should make the clinician more alert. Most parents, quite naturally, seek the help of their physician for these symptoms.

Some general discussion of somatization is necessary although each illness has its own special pathology. According to Alexander (1950), in somatization reactions the emotional stress, i.e. anxiety or hostility, is relieved by channeling the original impulse through the autonomic nervous system creating a pathophysiological environment with changes in motor activity and blood supply. Long continued dysfunction may finally lead to actual structural changes. For example, the ulcer itself has no psychologic significance. The hyper-or hyposecretion, motility changes, blood supply changes are significant resultants of psychologic factors. What is striking, too, is that the patient does not consciously experience the emotion. It becomes *shortcircuited* through the autonomic system into visceral (and other) expression of various types.

Search for a single cause is fallacious (Silverman, 1971; Engel,

1962). It is doubtful that there are ulcer types, coronary types, etc., however seductive such a concept is. The organ choice or specificity of symptom complex problems are much discussed and there is no clear cut agreement. The most reasonable prevailing view is that typical conflict situations may tend to the production of psychosomatic reactions in a setting of various kinds of personality structures. Multiple factors need to be considered, especially genetic ones that are to be understood in biochemical terms. Others are developmental ones with the extraordinary variety of life experiences and situations and coping mechanisms. "Response to stress, whether physical or mental, differs at different ages, and consequences that occur later in life as a result of stress will be determined by what the individual's early experience has been as well as by innate factors." Silverman, p. 21). A given set of dynamic factors in one person does not mean that this same set of dynamic factors will produce precisely the same somatic problem in another person. There are ever so many variables.

The probability is that the disposition to react with a psychosomatic disorder is rooted in the specific mother-child relationship of early life. Psychoanalysts stress from their clinical studies the need for mother "to keep her child in lifelong dependency for the satisfaction of vital emotional and bodily needs." (Sperling, 1961). The child is in unconscious compliance with mother's needs to be sick and dependent. Mother appears to reject the child when well which is equated with assertion of independence and to reward him when he is sick which is equated with submitting to her wishes. The psychosomatically ill adolescent suffers, not mental pain or anxiety, but in the bodily suffering which avoids mental pain or anxiety.

Hunger is accompanied by hypermotility, hyperemia and hyperacidity of the stomach. The frustrated infant may set the pattern for the adolescent or man who so reacts when overcome with longing for something he cannot get and thus create the setting for an ulcer. The air passages of the upper respiratory tract may be shut by congestion and washed by excess secretion. *Misuse* of this reaction through early conditioning may lead later to neurotic vasomotor rhinitis and accentuate asthma. A common stimulus to disorders of the bowel seems to be bereavement. Stanley

Cobb (1950) formulated the concept of mediation of grief through the visceral archicortex and hypothalamus to the sacral ganglion leading to a hyperactive colon, producing colitis, which leads to further hyperactivity. To repeat, the direct effect of psychologic factors is the pathophysiology, not the structural change.

A discussion of some of the commoner and more specific psychosomatic disorders seen in adolescents follows.

Anorexia nervosa is a serious condition most often seen in adolescent girls and rarely in boys. In anorexia nervosa the adolescent has *voluntarily* stopped eating, lost much weight which is indeed visible, and there is concomitant amenorhea. The clinical picture is one of depression and of great resistance to treatment, medical or psychiatric. They have a high regard for keeping slim, and don't want to become women with breasts which are equated with sexiness. They wish to remain little girls, express disgust with sex, are preoccupied with thoughts about the abdomen, breasts, pregnancy. The entire family becomes embroiled in the anxiety about the weight, cachectic appearance, eating. The history usually shows that they have been overweight or even obese before the eating ceases, and after the anorexia is resolved many become overweight or even obese. They control the family with their non-eating and attempt to control the physician as well.

Refusal to eat is a common symptom in depression, and anorexia nervosa is often considered the equivalent of depression. It is far more than that. Menses have usually ceased. The emaciated appearance is a denial of femininity, is scarcely designed to attract males and thus is a defense against sexual temptations. Intensive work with anorexic adolescents has demonstrated sadistic desires to destroy through eating and so eating is avoided. At times there is a nearly psychotic hatred of the mother and a harsh punitive attitude toward the body which threatens to be female like mother. Inquiry often discloses exposure to frightening or too seductive contact with father or other men. It's dangerous to be a woman. With starvation and its consequences there is no need to worry about men, marriage, or pregnancy. One of the theories the young child has about birth is that mother eats a seed. Eating food can play into pregnancy fantasies and fears in anorexia as well as obesity.

Case: Sara, a 15 year old only child, was referred for refusing to eat to the point where the family physician considered hospitalization. He had stated that unless she was over 85 pounds he would do this. Sara carefully remained at 85½ pounds. She was an attractive, very thin, depressed teenager, highly intelligent and only mildly cooperative. A straight A student, she apparently was most meticulous and took a great deal of time to complete her homework. Menses began at age 13 and had been regular; secondary sexual development was present. She was moderately plump and, as it happens in this instance, her parents and family physician were very weight conscious. Sara decided to lose 15 pounds some six months ago to get down to 108-110 pounds to look more beautiful. She lost weight with a vengeance and menses ceased.

Meal times were battlefield about eating. Cajolery, threats, pleading, ignoring and bribing were employed with no success. The doctor unfortunately became involved in the bargaining too with the baseline weight under which she would be hospitalized. Both parents were very attached to Sara and mother was an especially high strung, volatile, phobic woman who had read a great deal of psychology and managed to sexualize virtually every symptom or act.

Sara told me in a weak voice she thought she was beautiful. She'd like boy friends but couldn't understand why she didn't appeal to them. The doctor's claim that about 108 pounds was her normal weight she regarded as a myth and besides she was 85¼ pounds and that was enough. She expressed rage against mother's inconsistency and outbursts, high regard for father who was most loving and supportive, wondered what a psychiatrist could do for her since she could solve her problems and was not concerned about anything. She was increasingly resistive in treatment, manipulative, angry, and just as she controlled eating, she stopped talking. Losing control to her meant both a total loss of eating control to the point of gross obesity and becoming a feminine woman. Then she feared loss of control and acting out her sexual fantasies. Intellectually, she expressed no aversion about sexual matters or pregnancy.

The writer persuaded the family and the doctor to make it clear indeed that eating or not eating was indeed entirely up to her. The doctor was urged to set no limits but to make it clear that since she had a medical condition he was not going to bargain about exact weights and if her condition did not improve, just as with other medical conditions, he would take whatever necessary steps even to hospitalization to remedy this. It was up to her. She reluctantly began to eat and after a rocky, testing start, gradually gained weight. Gradually, too, she resumed the usual life of a 16 year old continuing treatment with another psychiatrist when the writer had to be away for a long period of time.

In anorexia nervosa the medical approach alone rarely resolves the problem. It is wise for the physician to request psychiatric consultation and treatment when necessary. Both psychiatrist and clinician work together.

Asthma, Allergy, Skin Disorders, Migraine. Anxiety precipitates or exaggerates an asthma attack; it does not cause it. Where the breathing difficulty is severe, anxiety is heightened and the attack may become even more severe. Separation from the care of a maternal or protective person is a central factor in the precipitation of the attack. Rage and anxiety ("choking with rage") have led to severe attacks of bronchial asthma. Actually it is the threat of separation that largely produces the anxiety and rage. The adolescent struggles between the wish for freedom and the need to have the protective support of a maternal person. Asthmatic attacks often lessen when the doctor or a familiar person appears. In one local asthma clinic a number of teenage girls were seen repeatedly in virtual status asthmaticus after rows with their mothers. Literally, these girls were *choking with rage* and treatment involved individual and family therapy where the family would cooperate.

It is essential for the physician to investigate the family life of the adolescent asthmatic and particularly his relationship to his mother. Where there is unusual dependency on the part of the youth or an overcontrolling or rejecting mother the speculation that psychological factors play a role is reasonable.

Where there are obvious conflicts swirling around and involving the adolescent, the physician must, as part of his treatment, make the time and effort to resolve these in addition to any medical regimen which will reduce and control the asthma. If he cannot do so, psychiatric evaluation and help should be sought. This will not cure the asthma. It will reduce the stresses giving rise to this frightening symptom. Nor should the adolescent be made an invalid. Indeed he should be encouraged to participate in all reasonable activities even if a little wheezing does occur. Of course, the physician is the final judge in this decision. (Schneer, 1963).

Anxiety may exaggerate allergic attacks such as swelling of the throat, eyelids, face, and of course, wheezing. Allergic phenomena may appear in adolescence and these need to be evaluated like any other allergic condition regardless of the psychological milieu. One 15 year old girl appeared to have swelling of the face and throat whenever she was enraged at her mother. She could only rarely express angry feelings toward anyone, and especially towards mother with whom she was closely intertwined. When enraged, her throat swelled. She often felt depressed when mother's mood was such that she isolated the adolescent. Her face and lids would swell and often itchy rashes would appear on her arms and back. The swelling might well be the weeping of depression. Nonetheless, care and desensitization by an allergist was essential together with psychiatric help. While these are the presenting symptoms there is usually a complex assortment of problems as well. (Harms, 1963).

Neurodermatitis is not uncommon in adolescence and readily leads to excoriations with unsightly disfigurement. Eva's mother was always afraid Eva was going to die and whatever disease she read about she would have Eva examined for that disease. Mother stated she breathed and lived for Eva, a depressed, passive, isolated, bright, likable 17 year old. After falling in love with a male teacher who was kind to her and about whom she had sexual fantasies, an itching rash appeared on her legs, arms and occasionally her face. She enjoyed scratching; it made her feel better. She wanted to be stroked by him but could not realize her fantasies. She dug into her skin. She related she must be ugly; otherwise why were not her wishes gratified. She literally disfigured herself to protect herself against acting sexually and to punish herself for these fantasies. Lotions relieve the itching but without resolving the underlying psychopathology the condition is nagging, persistent, uncomfortable and disfiguring. If the physician or dermatologist can comfortably explore the problems behind the symptom, that is certainly indicated. If the neurodermatitis persists, psychiatric consultation should be sought.

Migraine often makes its appearance in adolescence and may be more common around the time of menses. Extreme tension or anxiety but certainly hostility are the dynamic forces precipitating such an attack. Obviously not every rageful person develops a migraine for there are many other facets to this troublesome problem. The treatment of migraine is both medical and psychological where every effort must be made to uncover the hostility and to help with healthier coping mechanisms. (Ostfeld, 1963). Sally described an attack as follows. She would have *sick* feelings, then a dull headache. This might go on for several days with an anxious feeling. Seemingly suddenly there would be a blurring of vision or spots before her eyes with extreme sensitivity to light, and then a crashing pain, and the full attack would appear. The migraine attacks in adolescents do not appear to be as classical in description as is the case with adults. Sally could never permit herself to express anger. Love and approval were obtained by emotional suppression. She was a most ambitious girl, striving for success and precocity to gain mother's applause. She recognized how overcontrolled and perfectionistic she was, the latter most evident in her school work. An *overload* of stimuli such as menses, responsibilities, disappointment in her boy friend, jealousy of her friends and disapproval from mother often set the stage for an attack.

Menstrual Disturbances. Any girl who has not menstruated by the age of 15 years deserves a medical examination. While primary amenorrhea, a total absence of menstruation, usually has organic causes, it is not uncommon in girls who attempt to deny their femininity. Jane's menses did not begin until age 16. Despite very obvious secondary sexual characteristics she resented being a girl. She was a fine baseball player, did not wear dresses, and when swimming wore extremely binding tops in an effort to hide breast development. Her family doctor's discussions helped her so that menses soon began but her problems around sexuality finally led her to seek psychiatric help.

Secondary amenorrhea may be due to pregnancy, chronic illness, malnutrition, anorexia nervosa, obesity and a wide variety of emotional disturbances. It is usually not wise to induce menses with hormones unless there is a clearly defined endocrine condition. Correction of the emotional or physical disturbance will be accomplished by renewal of menses. Irregular menses, too, may have its emotional basis but if bleeding is prolonged or irregular, prompt medical evaluation is imperative. Reaction to pelvic examination by the adolescent girl varies. Most are very sensitive about it but most cooperate if it is medically necessary and the physician is considerate and tactful. A judgmental or condemning attitude is unwarranted and offensive to the adolescent girl who will refuse.

Dysmenorrhea and pre-menstrual tension are common. Most girls complaining of menstrual cramps are free of pelvic disorders. Explanations that the cramps are physiologic, discussion of the process of menstruation, together with symptomatic relief is helpful. To say they are imaginary is absurd; the cramps are a reality to the girl suffering from them. To help the family help the adolescent to avoid becoming invalided at menses time is an important consideration. Troubled, nervous, tense girls appear more likely to have menstrual cramps. Many girls, or more often their parents, notice tension pre-menstrually. Those who have difficulty with the feminine role often have a disgust for menstruation, try to hide the fact they are menstruating and more usually have cramps the first or second day of menses. These adolescents may require special help to accept their feminine role.

Before proceeding to a discussion of obesity, a major problem for the adolescent when it exists, mention must be made of a variety of disorders. The *adolescent diabetic* requires constant care and can never recover. Many a conflict with parents is fought by refusal to take insulin, repeated admissions for diabetic coma, and just generally indifferent control of the diabetes. Tina was an attractive, brilliant girl who was referred because of repeated episodes of diabetic coma, indifferent attention to her

medical regimen, and the beginning presence of diabetic retino-
pathy. Tina was very depressed, enraged at fate and heredity and
therefore her parents, and adamantly refused treatment. Suicidal
ideation was suspected which, while she denied, she acted out in
her lack of care for herself. She died a year or two later after becoming blind. It is so important for the adolescent diabetic to be
informed about his illness, prospects for marriage, children, trans-
mission of the diabetes, and to be encouraged to take full responsibility for his own care. Any tendency to be invalided by parents or significant others must be stopped. Any indication that
conflicts are being enacted in the lack of care must be dealt with
swiftly; the family must usually be involved. Consultation with a
psychiatrist will be valuable and if the situation is serious, help
for the adolescent and his family may well be life saving.

Peptic ulcer is not infrequent in children and adolescents. In
a preliminary investigation prior to research of attempted suicide
in adolescents, the first eleven males had a history of peptic ulcer.
The writer was not able to validate this finding in the controlled
studies. Careful histories of adolescents with peptic ulcer uni-
formly demonstrate an unrequited demand for love and attention
either not supplied or insufficiently supplied in infancy. Stress
situations replicating the needs and frustrations of early infancy
lead to the pathological physiology which in turn may lead to the
structural changes. Of course, medical treatment is the first concern. Should every peptic ulcer patient receive psychiatric help?
Every adolescent should be helped when necessary to achieve autonomy and the capacity to fulfill his needs in his relationships
with his peers and with his parents in a new, filial, non-dependent
role. This should be the guideline as to whether or not to recommend psychological help (Mirsky, 1958).

Mucous colitis and *ulcerative colitis* are difficult problems.
Ulcerative colitis is a serious intestinal condition and there are
many case reports of the help psychiatrists have been able to render children and adolescents. The medical management is primary. The gut *spits* out its internalized rage in its symptomatology. Psychological studies of *mucous colitis* indicate a variety of
dynamic forces behind the problem. The fecal discharge is a discharge of sexual and aggressive impulses through a somatic symp-

tom. This protects against anxiety stemming from one's own destructiveness. The symptom is symbolically devaluing a frustrating mother to feces and the fecal discharge is equivalent to giving her up. The physical suffering of the diarrhea is the punishment for the sadistic impulses. Always, the medical management is of primary importance and psychological help for the young person is indicated. (Engel, 1958; Sperling, 1957).

A most troublesome problem is *obesity*. Not only is the adolescent encased in a wall of fat but there is almost invariably much parental concern, anger, scorn, derision and conflict. Simply put, all cases are related to the fact that food and eating are used to appease non-nutritional needs and tensions "which are erroneously interpreted as 'desire to eat.' " (Bruch, 1971, p. 271). All parents of fat adolescents are extremely weight conscious, have often been fat and struggle to maintain their weight, and are experts in dietary values and reducing exercises.

The history of the obese adolescent will usually show that the young person never or rarely experienced relief of frustration, tension, anxiety that normal nursing provides for the infant which may be due to many factors such as mother's illness, scheduled routine care or separations at an early age. Repeatedly, it has been stated that severing infantile ties is a major task in adolescence. In early adolescence, particularly upon separation from the mother such as boarding school or even camp, overeating is common. The fat adolescent is often an object of derision, is unhappy, depressed, has usually had a long history of diets and being dieted and frequently feels quite hopeless. Eating is not a response to hunger only. Any stress can be channeled into eating.

The psychological factors underlying obesity are varied but it does not mean that these factors always produce obesity. Food has defensive purposes. After all, food is the primary indication of being loved and valued. Access to the maternal breast assures infantile relief of frustration and discomfort in the infant. Food has symbolic meanings too. Its ingestion may be the incorporation of the parent as a love object, or the cannabilistic incorporation of the person of the mother, or hostile feelings toward siblings or father. As noted earlier, the child thinks a baby is made by mother eating a seed. Obesity may be a resultant of unconscious pregnancy fantasies, even in males. Fatness is a defense against sexual association. Fat means ugly. Being fat and ugly the girl need not fear dating nor is she in any way a competitor with mother. Where this dynamic is present, the mothers are quite weight conscious, slim and attractive. The various unconscious tensions often produce great guilt feelings, i.e. cannibalistic fantasies, pregnancy fantasies and aggression is directed against the self, producing depression and more eating. In most girls studied by the writer there was much internalized rage usually toward mother with depression and eating to "feel better." Eating is devouring and symbolically reducing the object of rage to waste. (Mohr, 1958).

Obese adolescents often say they are addicted to food; they are not hungry. All want quick results. There is little tolerance for frustration or anxiety. After stuffing themselves they do not feel satisfied. They eat at odd hours, or alone, or at night and frequently keep up a pretense of dieting by eating sparingly at the dinner-table. Eating binges are like temper tantrums, or filling a pit of depression, or subduing a fierce rage. Rarely do they express anger; they need to be liked. Craving for sweets is common in adolescents but the fat ones do not get fat just on sweets. The concoctions described as eaten would drive any usual eater out of the kitchen with a feeling of awe at the enormous quantity and nausea at the dish or sandwich. Obesity is destructive physically and psychologically but being fat does offer solutions to many difficulties. It is hard to give up such a basic solution.

The following cases will illustrate much of the above. Gina was 100 pounds overweight. At the age of 18 months she was abruptly weaned, cried inconsolably for days and reverted to sucking her fingers. Her parents stated she began to overeat since then and from age four on she was repeatedly dieted by pediatricians, in sanitaria and must have lost and gained hundreds of pounds. As a teenager she was cajoled, bribed, threatened and sent off on trips. Once father promised her $1000 for each pound lost. She promptly lost 10 pounds so she could spend a few months in Europe. Gina would *sneak eat* and liked to eat soft, mushy foods often loading whatever she ate with mayonnaise to make it softer and *gooey*. She loved to talk and smoked incessantly. Incidentally, with the huge weight gain menses had ceased.

Psychotherapy revealed a hungry, needy, easily depressed attractive girl. The obesity symptom said to her mother, "Look, I'm not your competitor. I'm fat and ugly." Mother was a petite, very attractive woman. Gina and father adored one another. Her fatness helped her to avoid dating, maintain the facade of a sweet, obliging girl. Her rage was intense as revealed in dreams and fantasies where she destroyed mother. Frustration, fury, guilt drove her to eating binges lasting for days. At times when she longed for sweetness or dreamed of a loving, nurturing mother, her lips would swell to which she associated how she would like to suck on a mother's breast. With prolonged treatment, Gina eventually followed a sensible medical regimen and gradually lost weight among many other changes.

Bea, at 17, was everybody's pal, boys and girls. Actually, she was a very lonely, depressed girl who became progressively heavier as adolescence approached. She did not date and the friction between mother and herself was marked. Father called her a "fat cow;" mother constantly scolded about her heaviness. She would sarcastically state, "Whenever I see you, your backside is protruding from the refrigerator." Bea was in a state of constant fury at mother and frequently at father. She would say nothing but run into the kitchen and eat whatever was edible. She longed for a beau but she said to the writer she was too much woman for a young man, referring to her weight. At times mother would be troubled and Bea nurtured her. Then she felt close, weight gain would cease and anger would subside. Parents were helped to make the overeating Bea's problem and not interfere. Bea soon recognized the stressful events which led her to the kitchen, and with emotional nutrition from parents, peers, boys, and recognition of creativeness, she gradually lost weight. At first, there were lapses but when she went to college she maintained a reasonable weight.

Therapy of the obese youth is psychological and medical. The family must be involved and cooperative especially if the young person lives at home. Then the problem is made the young person's and once engaged in therapy they are most interesting to work with and quite responsive. When an adolescent is forced into therapy but not involved in it, little can be accomplished. It can be a malignant problem with some who have deep psychological problems and refuse to come to grips with them.

SUMMARY

There is no specific constellation of stresses or dynamic factors that each time will produce a specific symptom. There are many variables including genetic factors. The adolescent with somatic symptoms converts his suffering into physical symptoms. He suffers from his physical manifestations. The clinician must be aware of this, and guide his treatment accordingly. The family must be helped too. When in doubt, consultation with a psychiatrist can be of much value to the physician and, certainly, with the serious problems. i.e. anorexia nervosa, ulcerative colitis, psychiatric help is a part of the total patient care.

Affection in itself will not bring an adolescent close to the clinician or therapist. It may do just the opposite; it may suggest weakness. An adolescent who feels he can outsmart the physician or therapist usually will have little use for him. The ability to treat adolescents implies much experience with them, an intimate knowledge of their habits, weaknesses and strengths. Not every adolescent disturbance is equally well treated by the same therapist. The empathy and spontaneous relatedness to the adolescent's feeling of life is much more than mere understanding and insight. It is this empathy which eases treatment contact. The therapist shares the young person's emotions and fantasies, but with a restraint that helps the adolescent to identify himself with the therapist and hence guides him toward insight, which in turn helps him develop his standards and a sense of self. Adolescence is a time of psychological and social self-finding.

The therapist must be free of anxiety, which he cannot be if he is unfamiliar with adolescents, or if he fears he may be overlooking significant material requiring attention, or if real emotional conflicts in his own adolescence have been unsatisfactorily resolved. The problem for every therapist is how limited he may be in the type of patient he can work with by his own personality make-up or life experiences. The easy display of feelings, the ingenuity necessary to make therapy interesting enough to be continued, the abilities to shift from dramatizing to interpretation, from support to demand, from humor to surprise—these are not qualities every therapist possesses, nor can every therapist acquire them.

No one can say that treating an adolescent is not challenging or difficult or rewarding or frustrating or irritating. It is always interesting and requires a flexibility of technique as well as a supple, well enlightened personality applying the techniques. The therapist's tolerance for frustration must be high indeed! Many clinicians have learned much of the above and apply these principles. But they also know their limitations and degree of competence and do refer the adolescent to the specialist for his special knowledge, experience and expertness (Teicher, 1959).

BIBLIOGRAPHY

1. Alexander, F.: *Psychosomatic Medicine.* Norton, New York, 1950.
2. Bruch, H.: Juvenile obesity: its course and outcome. *Int Psychiat Clin,* 7:231-254,
3. Bruch, H.: Obesity in Adolescence. In Howells, G.S., (Ed.): *Modern Perspectives in Adolescent Psychiatry,* Brunner-Mazel, New York, p. 254-273, 1971.
4. Cobb, S.: *Emotions and Clinical Medicine.* Norton, New York, 1950.
5. Engel, G. L.: *Psychological Development in Health and Development.* Saunders, 1962.
6. Engel, G. L.: Studies of ulcerative Colitis V. psychological aspects and their implications for treatment. *Amer J Dig Dis, 3:*315, 1958.
7. Group for Advancement of Psychiatry, *Normal Adolescence.* V. 6, February 1968.
8. Harms, E., (ed.): *Somatic and Childhood Aspects of Childhood Allergies.* Macmillan, New York, 1963.
9. Harris, H. I.: The Range of Psychosomatic Disorders in Adolescence. In *Modern Perspectives in Adolescent Psychiatry,* Howells, G. J., (Ed.): Brunner-Mazel, New York, p. 237-253, 1971.
10. Mirsky, I. A.: Physiologic psychologic and social determinants in the etiology of duodenal ulcer. *Amer J Dig Dis, 3:*285, 1958.
11. Mohr, G.: *The Stormy Decade: Adolescence.* Random House, New York, 1958.
12. Ostfeld, A. M.: *The Common Headache Syndromes.* Thomas, Springfield, 1963.

13. Schneer, H., (Ed.): *The Asthmatic Child*. Harper & Row, New York, 1963.
14. Silverman, S.: *Psychological Aspects of Physical Symptoms*. Appleton-Century-Crofts, New York, 1971.
15. Sperling, M.: Psychoanalytic treatment of ulcerative Colitis. *Internat J Psychoanal, 37*:1, 1957.
16. Sperling, M.: Psychosomatic Disorders in Adolescents. In Lorand, S., and Schneer, H., *Psychoanalytic Approach to Problems and Therapy*. Hoeber, New York, p. 202-216, 1961.
17. Teicher, J.: Psychotherapy of adolescents. *Calif Med, 90*:29-31, January 1959.

CHAPTER 4

THE ADOLESCENT AND HIS RELATION TO AUTHORITY

MALVINA W. KREMER, M.D.

PROBLEMS OF ADOLESCENTS and authority appear to be at least as old as recorded history. In the golden age of classical antiquity Greek writers complained of the bad manners and lack of respect on the part of adolescents in terms that are reminiscent of articles in today's newspapers and magazines. The folklore of nations and tribes, great and small, contains many stories of conflict between youth and age. The biblical injunction "Honor thy father and thy mother," must have filled a need in ancient times as in our own.

Two contrasting themes may be discerned in the legends. On the one hand, youth is strong, impetuous, innovative, often heroic; age is slow, crafty, resistive to change, often tyrannical. On the other hand, youth may be depicted as hasty, rash, sometimes foolish, while age is deliberate, planful and wise. We can easily recognize that these contrasting themes reflect, on the one hand, the conservatism which gives continuity and stability to a culture or society and, on the other hand, the need for development and change without which the culture or society would stagnate and perish. We can easily recognize that these themes describe the contemporary scene also. There is, however, an important new element. The old struggles were mostly for riches, territory, power or love. They took place within an established framework of relationships and all protagonists shared a common system of values which gave meaning to the goals of the struggle. Without explicitly saying so, youth was endorsing the wisdom of the elders by accepting and trying to take over these goals. What is new, is that today youth doubts the wisdom of the elders. Our young people contemplate the world around them and their doubt turns into active mistrust. They hold their elders responsible for the injustices, wars and the threat of atomic annihilation that hangs over all of us. The young people today question the institutions and value systems which permitted such a state of affairs to occur and they are but little impressed by the results of adult efforts to improve matters.

These ideas deserve more extended consideration and elaboration than I can give them here. I have stated them briefly at the outset because in the contemporary psychiatric tradition the relationship of adolescents to authority is usually discussed in the framework of family structure, sexual development and rebellion against parents. Deviations from accepted behavior are seen primarily as the acting out of unresolved conflict and are taken as indicators of psychopathology. In many instances this may indeed be the case, but the contemporary rebellion is too widespread and too deep seated to be regarded as an expression of the vicissitudes of personal history. There are many different kinds of rebels and many different forms of rebellion. What we are witnessing is an unprecedented confluence of problems in the realm of individual psychodynamics and the broad sociological issues of our time.

The variety of rebels and rebellions defies simple classification. Some of the young people manifest familiar symptoms and fit easily into the standard diagnostic categories. Other cases cross the established diagnostic lines and do not fit easily under any one label. It is often difficult to apply the usual criteria of psychopathology. In the long run it will probably prove necessary to reexamine the diagnostic scheme and delineate new categories which will correspond more realistically to the kinds of patients we see. Eash case presents a complex mixture of elements which requires careful study. Without claiming to be exhaustive I will attempt to outline some of the items which I have found clinically useful in evaluating adolescent rebels.

Briefly stated, I look for the presence or absence of symptoms such as anxiety, fears, phobias, depression and thinking disturbances. Next I review the general level of functioning in other areas in addition to those for which consultation was sought. I make certain to investigate the family history and structure and the inter-relationships among the family members. I pay particular attention to the sequence and timing of symptoms and behavioral deviations. I make strenuous efforts to interview parents both to obtain information and to observe the interaction between them and with their adolescent. This outline may also help in judging when an acting-out adolescent should be referred to a psychiatrist.

As a general rule, adolescents do not often seek help for psychological problems. Usually they are sent for examination because their behavior has come to someone else's attention, for example, parents, schools, social agencies or the police. Even when they are aware of definite symptoms adolescents may not offer the information spontaneously during the examination. It is, therefore, necessary to make specific inquiry, though not always at the first interview. Many adolescents will be defensive about their symptoms so that careful, tactful and sympathetic probing may be needed. Some adolescents will regard the interview as a contest, while others will adopt a facade of conformity and give what they consider the expected conventional replies.

By pursuing the investigation, an impressive array of symptoms may be revealed. Underneath the defiance and rebellion one may find anxiety, depression, cynicism and a profound sense of hopelessness and despair.

It has been repeatedly stated that adolescence is a period of great stress in which emotional turmoil is the norm. According to this view a variety of symptoms may be anticipated but these do not have the same significance as they would in adults. My own experience suggests that turmoil and symptoms are not universal or inevitable. A study by Masterson indicates that when recognizable symptom complexes appear, they must be considered carefully.

Evaluation of the symptom picture is aided by consideration of the history and family background. Minor isolated symptoms tend to be associated with a *stable family* background and *positive relationships* among the members of the family. Conversely, more serious and pervasive symptomatology tend to be associated with disturbed family backgrounds characterized by frictions and disruption. A history of antagonisms between the parents, lack of emotional support for the child and hostility toward parents may help in determining whether the adolescent rebellion is derived from resistance to the parents.

The history of extrafamilial relationships may also cast some light on the nature of the rebellion. Here we look for resistance to authority in school and other institutional settings as well as relationships with peers and playmates. We look for earlier indications of capacity to deal with frustration and to control aggressive responses. In many instances the roots of later rebellion may be detected in the earlier experiences. The pattern of acting upon impulse, in conflict with or in disregard of, authority may be established early in life or it may represent a failure of integrative capacities in special stress situations. It is, therefore, important to inquire about the sequence of previous difficulties and any special circumstances which may have precipitated them. Families often have well established modes for dealing with problems or conflicts which cast the adolescent in a particular role. This situation may be evident from the patient's account or it may be necessary to find the clues in interviewing the parents.

I commented earlier that there is some doubt about the universality and inevitability of turmoil and symptoms in adolescents. There is no doubt, however, that adolescence is a period of major transformations and that adolescents face challenging tasks. In the face of the mounting physiological pressures of sexuality they must define their role in life, complete their education or training and emerge from their sheltered position in the family to assume independent adult responsibility. How well a given adolescent meets these challenges depends on many factors drawn from the entire range of his experience both intrafamilial and extrafamilial. Among the consequences of this experience there is one which has not, I believe, received sufficient emphasis. I refer to the sense of capability or competence to deal with the tasks and challenges. In stressing the sense of capability, I do not mean to minimize the sense of identity which has received much attention in recent years. Capability is an aspect of identity, but it is important enough to deserve separate mention. Neither do I mean to minimize the importance of the established patterns of defense or of the transferences which the adolescent brings into new situations. What I am trying to emphasize is that the sense of competence is a central factor in determining how the adolescent will deal with the tasks before him.

Identity and competence are in turn related to two additional points in the inventory of items that are useful in evaluating acting-out or rebellious adolescents. These are the adolescent's plans or goals and his motivation and his capacity for sustained effort. To have goals or plans requires that one should have a sense of one's self in relation to the surrounding world and some notion of how one might fit into this world. Motivation and sustained effort are facilitated by the expectation that one will be able to achieve the goals. It is difficult to have plans or sustain efforts to attain them if one does not have a sense of competence.

The adolescent's relationship to authority is, of course, profoundly influenced by his relationship to the primary authority figures, the parents, but it is equally influenced by his aims and expectations, by his conception of his role in the world and by his sense of competence to achieve what he desires. Goals, motivation and competence need not be explicitly formulated and few adolescents are able to make statements about these matters on request, but they are very real factors. If the overall summation of these factors is positive, the adolescent is likely to find a constructive relationship to authority which is not necessarily accepting or subservient. If he rebels it will be for worthwhile goals and the rebellion will be organized and planful. He will more easily maintain an appropriate balance in the different activities in his life and he will be less likely to extend the rebellion to the point of self-defeat. On the other hand, if the summation of goals, motivations and competence is negative the result is likely to be a sense of defeat that may be accompanied by bitterness, cynicism and despair. Such an adolescent is less likely to rebel along constructive lines. He may espouse worthwhile causes, but the underlying mood and affect will not be difficult to recognize. The rebellion is apt to be indiscriminate, poorly organized and in the long run self defeating. Such an adolescent will not merely object to an old fashioned curriculum but will drop out of school and learn nothing rather than learn what he considers irrelevant. If he is verbal and has had the advantages of an education, he may develop various theoretical and philosophical rationalizations for deviant behavior. If he is less intellectual and less verbal he simply drops out and acts out, through delinquency, addictions and perversions and so on.

To sum up, the most conspicuous feature of the current adolescent scene is the challenge to established authority and basic value systems long accepted without question. These developments cannot be regarded merely as psychopathology or aberrations arising from problems in personal development and family relationships, although the latter may play a part. By careful clinical examination it is possible to identify and evaluate the elements of personal psychopathology in any individual instance. It is equally important to identify the constructive elements in the youthful protestors and mobilize their energies toward constructive goals.

CHAPTER 5

DEPRESSION AND SUICIDE

James M. Toolan, M.D.

DURING THE PAST ten years many studies have been published on the possible biochemical basis of depression, and even more numerous are the publications on the response of depression to various antidepressant medications. The largest portion of this work has been concerned with adult patients. Little attention has been paid to depression in children and adolescents. Kanner's[21] *Child Psychiatry* and the first edition of the *American Handbook of Psychiatry*[3] do not mention the term in connection with children and adolescents. Neither Beck,[6] in a 370-page monograph on depression, nor Klerman,[26] in a review of clinical research on depression, cite a single paper on this topic.

How do we explain such a marked discrepancy in the attention paid to depressive reactions in adults as compared with those in children and adolescents? There are several factors responsible for this state of affairs. On purely theoretical grounds, some authors have concluded that depression does not occur in childhood (Rochlin[31]). Most observers have noted the absence in children of the usual clinical signs and symptoms that characterize depression in adults. Lehman[27] has succinctly summarized the picture of depression as commonly encountered: "There has always been agreement among clinicians about the phenomena that characterize the psychiatric condition which we call depression or sometimes melancholia. The characteristic symptoms are: a sad, despairing mood; decrease of mental productivity and reduction of drive; retardation or agitation in the field of expressive motor responses. These might be called the primary symptoms of depression. There are also secondary symptoms—feelings of helplessness; hypochondriacal preoccupations; feelings of depersonalization; obsessive-compulsive behavior; ideas of self-accusation and self-depreciation; nihilistic delusions; paranoid delusions; hallucinations; suicidal ruminations and tendencies." Such clinical pictures are rarely encountered in children and seldom seen in adolescents until fourteen or fifteen years of age. The scepticism concerning the existence of depression in childhood has been summarized by Rie,[30] who reviewed much of the literature on depression in children. He states: "An examination of the implications for child psychopathology of the dynamics of adult depression, including the roles of aggression, orality, and self-esteem, generates serious doubt about the wisdom of applying the concept of depression to children." He continues: "There may be room to believe that the fully differentiated and generalized primary affect characterizing depression, namely despair or hopelessness, is one of which children—perhaps prior to the end of the latency years—are incapable."

During the past decade several authors have concluded that depression is a definite clinical entity in children and in adolescents. Toolan,[37] in 1962 stated: "We have to cease thinking in terms of adult psychiatry and instead become accustomed to recognizing the various manifestations by which depression may be represented in younger people." This is a concept that is familiar to pediatricians, who have long recognized that some physical illnesses may be manifested differently in the pediatric patient than in the adult patient. As early as 1946 Spitz and Wolf[35] coined the phrase "anaclitic depression" to describe a syndrome observed in institutionalized infants. They describe these infants as showing symptoms of withdrawal, insomnia, weeping, weight-loss, and marked developmental retardation. Some of these infants failed to survive. The authors postulated that these were the presenting symptoms of a depression caused by separation from the mother between the sixth and eighth months of life, for at least a three-month period. It is of interest that they observed the severest reactions in those infants who had previously enjoyed a good relationship with the mother. Goldfarb,[17] writing in the same year on institutionalized children, described social and intellectual retardation as a result of emotional deprivation. However, he did not use the term depression.

In a well-known study, Engle and Reichsman[15] described in detail an infant with a gastric fistula who spontaneously became depressed and in whom they could experimentally induce a depressive reaction. After recovering from her initial depression, the infant would become withdrawn and depressed whenever confronted with strangers but would recover when a familiar person reentered her life. The authors theorize that this depression was due to the loss of the mother, and the infant's perception of her helpless state. This is very similar to the explanation for childhood depression presented by Sandler and Joffe.[32] Bowlby,[11] who has studied the effects of maternal separation from the child, describes three stages that ensue: Protest, Despair, and Detachment. Bowlby[11] uses the term "mourning" in referring to these three stages, although we would prefer to consider them as various stages of depression. Despert,[14] in reviewing her clinical experience, stated that 26 out of 400 children she had treated could be described as having ". . . depressive moods and/or evidencing preoccupation with suicide or expressing realistic suicidal threats." This led her to conclude that "Depression in children is not so uncommon as a survey of the literature would indicate."

Keeler[24] describes eleven children who reacted to the death of a parent with various manifestations of depression. It is of interest that he noted that clinicians often fail to recognize such depression because children not infrequently hide these feelings. He felt that psychological testing might therefore be of assistance. Bierman[9] et al. noted the case of a six-year-old boy, ill with acute poliomyelitis, who developed a severe depression. The authors stated that the youngster's appearance and behavior was similar to that exhibited by adult depressives. "He looked sad and depressed, so much so, that the interviewer was prompted to record that he had at times what one would call in an adult a melancholic facies. He talked in a low, weak, sad voice." Although the depression lasted for two months following his discharge from the hospital, the authors commented that the child ". . . said very little directly about his disability, but in his doll play and psychological test performance a great deal was revealed which bears on the topic of body damage and hence on the narcissistic injury. The extent and severity of the perceived damage far surpassed those of the disability as objectively measured." The authors postulated that this child had reacted to his illness with a lowered self-esteem, similar to the reaction of many adult melancholics.

Harrington and Hassan,[18] who were treating a number of eight to eleven-year-old females in outpatient therapy, mentioned that seven girls out of a group of fourteen were, in their opinion, depressed. They described ". . . a common syndrome of weeping bouts, some flatness of affect, fears of death for self or parents, irritability, somatic complaints, loss of appetite and energy, and varying degrees of difficulty in school adjustments." These authors also called attention to the similarity of the clinical picture usually seen in adult neurotic depressives. They theorized that self-depreciation and ego weakness were the important determinants.

Describing seven children from six to twelve years of age with school phobias, Agras[2] emphasized the relationship of school phobias to childhood depression. He felt that both mother and child were often depressed. He described ". . . a syndrome comprising depressive anxiety, mania, somatic complaints, phobic and paranoid ideation . . ." which he believed to be ". . . close phenomenologically to the depressive disorders of adults." Campbell[13] had previously mentioned the relationship of school phobias to depression in children, although he believed them to be a variety of manic-depressive disorders. Statten,[36] in studying homesickness in children, felt that these children were attempting to adjust to an underlying depression precipitated by their separation from home. Sperling,[34] in 1959, introduced the term "equivalents of depression" in children. She and Toolan[37] both emphasize that the clinical manifestations of depression in infants and children may differ significantly from the symptoms in adult patients. Both authors describe sleep difficulties, anorexia, gastrointestinal disorders such as ulcerative colitis, as indications of depression, especially in infants and young children. The authors also mention that the mothers of such children are often depressed.

Ling,[28] who studied a group of children with severe headaches, stated that ten out of twenty-five in this group were depressed. He also called attention to a significant family history of depression in these children.

Writing about the latency-age child, Toolan[37] described behavioral symptoms such as disobedience, temper tantrums, truancy, and running away from home as depressive equivalents. He stated: "The youngster is convinced that he is bad, evil, unacceptable. Such feelings lead him into antisocial behavior, which in turn only further reinforces his belief that he is no good. The youngster will often feel inferior to other children, and that he is ugly and stupid." Pre-adolescents may also exhibit similar behavior as a manifestation of an underlying depression. Youngsters of that age will frequently use denial as a means of avoiding their depressive feelings. Boys in our culture find it difficult to acknowledge that they are depressed, often viewing such feelings as proof that they are weak. In early adolescence depression may be evidenced by restlessness, boredom, a reluctance to be alone, and a continual searching for new activities. Many normal adolescents will exhibit such behavior, but one should always be suspicious of depression if these symptoms persist. Many adolescents describe feelings of isolation, emptiness, and alienation which are often manifestations of an underlying depression. The tendency of adolescents and young adults to group together in fraternities and communes may be an attempt to find relief from such feelings through mutual support. Many youngsters will utilize drugs or alcohol as a means of escape from their depressive feelings. They will often engage in sexual activity, frequently of a promiscuous nature, as a means of relieving these depressions. Such activity may be temporarily quite successful, but usually leads to guilt and further depression. It is well known that many teen-age girls become pregnant out of wedlock in an attempt to escape from depression.

Physicians should be aware that physical complaints may be a symptom of depression in adolescents, as they often are in adults. Fatigue and headaches are often presenting complaints. Fatigue which is present in the morning should especially make one suspect depression. Persistent hypochondriacal preoccupation in teen-agers as in adults should make the physician alert to the possibility of an underlying depression.

Individuals who are depressed often complain of difficulty in concentrating. Such complaints should not be taken lightly by teachers, guidance counselors, and physicians; otherwise we will find good students failing academically, often to the amazement of both faculty and parents. Such students understandably become discouraged and convinced that they are unable to successfully cope with their studies. This belief will further diminish their weakened self-esteem, and lead to increasing depression. In a study of dropouts from Harvard University, Nicoli[29] concluded: "Depression is by far the most frequent and the most significant causal factor in the decision to interrupt or terminate one's college experience." He related the depression to an ". . . awareness of a disparity between the ideal self as a uniquely gifted intellectual achiever and the real self as one of thousands of outstanding students struggling in a threateningly competitive environment. This awareness, gradual or abrupt, results in the clinical picture frequently observed in the dropout; feelings of lassitude, inadequacy, hopelessness, low self-esteem, and inability to study."

One of the questions still to be answered is what effect depression during adolescence may have upon future psychic functioning. Hill,[19] studying the association of childhood bereavement with suicidal attempts writes: "Suicide is significantly more common in depressed women who lost their fathers at age ten to fourteen, and to a lesser extent at fifteen to nineteen. Men and women whose mothers died in the first ten years of their lives also attempted suicide more often." Such a study strongly suggests that these children may well have become depressed following the death of a parent and continued to be depressed as adults. Some adolescents undoubtedly spontaneously recover from depressive feelings, but many we believe do not. One might speculate that some of these depressed adolescents may well become the severe depressives of the involutional years.

It is widely recognized that many adolescents will utilize denial and acting out as a means of avoiding depressive feelings.

Such acting-out behavior may lead to serious delinquency, as has been described by Kaufman[23]: "A crucial determinant (in delinquency) is an unresolved depression, which is the result of the trauma which these children have experienced." He notes further, "We consider the delinquent acts of taking and doing forbidden things or expressing resentment and hostility to the depriving world as the child's pathologic method of coping with the depressive nucleus." Burks and Harrison[12] have described aggressive behavior on the part of many delinquents as being a method of avoiding depression. Kaufman[23] has theorized that many delinquents have a severely impoverished self-image and a profound emptiness of ego, similar to the emtiness of the schizophrenic ego.

By mid-adolescence many youngsters will exhibit the classic signs and symptoms of adult depressives. In addition, such adolescents will often present a picture of confused self-identity. They will complain of feeling isolated, and of feeling unloved and unworthy. These youngsters at times appear to resent their parents and are often overtly rebellious. In reality, however, they are overly-dependent on their parents. When such youngsters separate from home and parents to enter college or military service they frequently experience a profound homesickness and depression. The separation from the parents, though consciously desired, is experienced as a loss of love and support in these cases.

Upon reviewing the history of depressed adolescents, one discovers that many of them had exhibited behavioral problems prior to the onset of their overt depressive symptoms. This would appear to substantiate the thesis that such depressive equivalents are manifestations of depression in younger persons. It is of interest that such behavioral problems tend to disappear when the frank clinical picture of depression developed.

A study of depression in children should include some comments on the incidence of manic-depressive psychosis in children and adolescents. There is almost unanimous agreement that manic-depressive reactions are extremely rare in children and adolescents. Kasanin and Kaufman[22] were able to find only four affective psychoses prior to sixteen years of age. They noted that the four cases developed their initial symptoms after fourteen years of age. Anthony and Scott[4] reviewed the literature on manic-depressive psychosis from 1864 to 1954, and stated that only three cases in late childhood qualified for such a diagnosis. They added one new case of their own where the initial symptoms presented at twelve years of age. Campbell,[13] however, has felt that children may often develop manic-depressive psychoses. To date his views have not been widely accepted. Clinicians will often encounter hyperactive and manic-like behavior in children and young adolescents, but careful clinical observation and testing will almost invariably indicate that these are either brain-damaged children or excited schizophrenics.

Because many depressed youngsters find it difficult to acknowledge and discuss depressive feelings, psychological testing may be most helpful. One must recognize, however, that the psychodiagnostic picture in children and adolescents is often different from that seen in adult depressives. In children and adolescents anger is often openly expressed while depressive feelings are in the background. Adult depressives tend to show a reverse of this picture. The Rorschach will often show a diminution of color response as well as images of body emptiness. On the WISC or WAIS we frequently find a higher performance than verbal score, which is also the reverse of that seen in adult depressives. Such a patterning may be seen in sociopaths, and may be related to the tendency toward acting out already described.

The study of depression in children and adolescents can be assisted by giving attention to the dreams and fantasies of such patients. Depressed youngsters, for example, may often dream of dead persons, usually relatives, beckoning them on to the world of the dead. In their dreams they are frequently attacked and injured. On many occasions they will have dreams of body emptiness or loss of various parts of their bodies. Such loss has been interpreted by Kaufman[23] and Toolan[37] as referring to a loss of a significant relationship rather than castration anxiety. Depressed young people often fantasize that they are unloved and unwanted, as well as having previously belonged to another family. Fantasies of running away from home and/or being dead are not infrequent. Accompanying the latter two fantasies is the recurring theme that someone, usually the parents, will be sorry for having treated them so badly.

Treatment

In a single chapter one can scarcely do justice to the many facets that influence the treatment of depressed youngsters. The planning of therapy for each youngster should of course be individualized and will be influenced by such factors as age, the clinical picture, the family composition, resources available, etc. Infants who are diagnosed as presenting a picture of anaclitic or infantile depression require immediate alteration of their living arrangements. These infants require one significant person to care for them, preferably the mother if possible. Spitz and Wolf[35] have warned us that such infants may fail to recover if their depressions last more than three months. It is even more important to remember, however, that these reactions are preventable. Infants particularly, as well as children, should be separated from their mothers or mother surrogates only when absolutely necessary. Mothers should be allowed to care for and feed them while they remain in the hospital. Infants who require institutionalization, for example those awaiting adoption, should have one particular person assigned to them to act as mother surrogate.

Children and young adolescents who exhibit behavioral difficulties as a manifestation of depression are in general quite difficult therapeutic problems. As a rule, therapeutic programs for such youngsters should be similar to those appropriate to acting-out youngsters in general. The major difficulty, of course, is that such patients, and frequently their parents, do not feel that they are in need of assistance and as a result tend to blame their difficulties on others. These patients are usually referred by the schools, courts, and correctional agencies. Psychotherapy, as might be expected, is a most difficult task as these youngsters not only fail to recognize their need for help but use mechanisms of projection and denial to avoid facing their inner feelings of depression, isolation, and emptiness. The first task of the therapist, therefore, is to help the youngster to realize that he is unhappy and that his behavior is simply a symptom of his depression. Open confrontation and premature interpretation usually prove futile, and often frighten the patient into terminating treatment. Therefore the therapist must exhibit patience and understanding and allow the patient to face his depressive feelings when he is able to do so. These youngsters will often provoke and test the therapist, as they are convinced that no one can care for them. Many such youngsters have the infantile notion that they should be loved regardless of how they behave. Although these patients at times appear very desirous of a close therapeutic relationship, this may prove threatening to them. Either consciously or unconsciously they may fear the loss of such relationship, since they have lost other significant persons in their lives. When therapy does prove effective there will be a diminution of acting-out behavior, but this will often be followed by the appearance of an overt depression which will require an alteration of therapeutic technique.

The therapeutic approach toward the frankly depressed adolescent presents a different set of problems. Since many of these youngsters are suicidal the therapist may feel burdened and/or frightened by his responsibility, and as a result may recommend hospitalization when such is not necessarily indicated. Such patients, because they feel helpless, lethargic, and listless, may cause the therapist to react with boredom and impatience. Some therapists find it difficult to listen to a constant recital of hurt, unhappy, angry feelings. There is also the risk that some therapists may be unduly sympathetic and thus unwittingly encourage the patient to continue to behave in the same fashion as a means of gaining attention and affection.

The essence of all successful psychotherapy is the relationship between the patient and the therapist. This is especially true for the depressed adolescent, for he must be able to believe in the therapist when all his previous experiences have taught him to be suspicious of people. These depressed youngsters will often vacillate between trust and distrust of the therapist for a considerable period of time. Since they feel unworthy and unloved, it is very difficult for these depressed patients to believe that anyone can truly care for them. At the same time they may be unusually demanding of the therapist's time and attention, needing frequent reassurance. One positive factor is that these youngsters, unlike the younger acting-out depressed child, realize that they are unhappy and usually desire help. It is ironic, however, that they must often convince others, such as parents, physicians, and teachers, that they are depressed and that they require professional assistance. Many a young person has been dismissed as having *growing pains* or may be told to "pull yourself together and stop feeling sorry for yourself." Often a suicide attempt on the part of a depressed adolescent may be viewed as an attempt to convince others, and at times himself, that his problems are serious and that he requires assistance in their solution.

In my opinion most depressed adolescents require intensive therapy. Techniques such as suggestion, reassurance, support, and/ or environmental manipulation may appear to be beneficial, but all too often follow-up will reveal that the improvement has been short-lived and the patient has again become depressed. I do not recommend placement away from home unless the risk of suicide is great and/or the home situation is unduly destructive. It is imperative that the parents be actively involved in any therapeutic program. Such parents need assistance so that they can understand how their child feels, how their behavior may affect their child, and how to handle their own feelings of guilt and responsibility. Many therapists for these reasons recommend family therapy. It is, however, too early at this time to evaluate the effectiveness of this new approach as compared with the results of concurrent therapy with both child and parents.

As already mentioned, there have been numerous studies of the effects of antidepressant medication. There appears to be widespread agreement that such medication is often effective in treating adult depressives. Depressed children and adolescents, however, do not appear to respond as favorably. One might theorize that young patients perhaps metabolize these drugs differently from the older patient. Upon closer observation it would appear that those youngsters who present with a clear-cut picture of overt depression may respond favorably to antidepressant medication. Youngsters who exhibit behavioral difficulties as a manifestation of an underlying depression seldom respond favorably to antidepressant medication. Ling,[28] in his recent study of head-aches in children, has reported that these children did respond favorably to antidepressant medication. His patients varied in age from four to sixteen years.

There appear to be relatively few reports on the use of electro-convulsive therapy for the treatment of depressed children and adolescents. Over the last decade many groups have discontinued use of ECT even for adult depressions, except in those cases where antidepressant medication has been unsuccessful or where the risk of suicide was so great as to preclude the use of this medication because of its time-lag. We would recommend the use of ECT in children and adolescents be limited to those who present a clinical picture of frank depression, and then only when psychotherapy and antidepressant medication have proved ineffective.

Discussion

One may fairly draw the conclusion that while young children do not evidence depressive reactions similar to those seen in adults, the adolescent from fourteen years of age on often does so. We must ask if this is due to the fact that the younger child does not become depressed or does he evidence his depression in a different fashion? It is obvious from the literature cited in this paper that there is no agreement on this point. It would appear upon close study that children do become depressed but manifest it differently from adults. The controversy in many ways is reminiscent of the controversy over the existence of schizophrenia in children, twenty years ago. At the time it was maintained by many psychiatrists, especially those of an analytic persuasion, that children could not become schizophrenic. It is now widely acknowledged that many children present with a schizophrenic illness, even though the clinical picture varies considerably from that seen in the adult schizophrenic. We might also take note that the clinical picture of childhood schizophrenia begins to resemble that of the adult schizophrenic somewhere in mid to late adoles-cence. Let us not overlook the fact that the child is constantly developing and it is not surprising, therefore, that the clinical picture will vary greatly with the various developmental and maturational levels of the child. Clinicians should beware lest their clinical judgment be unduly influenced by theoretical formulations that may be open to question. As Boulanger[10] has stated: "A psychoanalyst may very well be reluctant to perceive in a child the equivalent of an adult's melancholia, for he is beseiged at once by all the points of theory which are unsettled and passionately disputed within the school: the organization and function of the ego, superego, and object relationships, the origin of the Oedipus complex and the complexities of the instinctual development, the purpose of masochism, and the validity of the death instinct."

Abraham[1] and Freud[16] in their classic papers on depression theorized that depression was a result of a punitive, harsh, superego, turning hostility and aggression against itself. They felt that the depressed person had identified with the ambivalently-loved, lost object. Both authors stressed the oral components of depression. Klein[25] has written extensively on the depressive position of childhood, which she considers to be a normal developmental stage for all infants. This theory has not received widespread acceptance. More recently psychoanalysts have theorized that depression is a result of the loss of a significant love-object, whether this loss occurs in fantasy or reality. Bibring[8] has emphasized the role that self-esteem plays in understanding depression. He states: "Depression can be defined as the emotional expression of a state of helplessness and powerlessness of the ego, irrespective of what may have caused the breakdown of the mechanism which established his self-esteem." He indicates that the basic mechanism is ". . . the ego's shocking awareness of its helplessness in regard to its aspirations."

As a result of Bibring's[8] contribution, the concept of the role of self-esteem in depression has assumed great significance. This has led Rie[30] to ask at what age a child may express feelings that can be called low self-esteem. He believes that the child is unable to experience a feeling of helplessness or diminished self-esteem until mid-adolescence at the earliest. In Rie's[30] opinion, "There may be reason to believe that the fully differentiated and generalized primary affect characterizing depression, namely despair or helplessness, is one of which children perhaps prior to the latency years, are incapable."

A recent paper by Sandler and Joffe,[32] modifying Bibring's[8] theory of the influence of self-esteem in depression, in my opinion answers the objection raised by Rie.[30] Sandler and Joffe[32] stress ". . . the basic biological nature of the depressive reaction, related to pain (and its opposite, *well-being*), rather than the psychologically more elaborate concept of self-esteem." They go on to say that depression ". . . can best be viewed as a basic psychobiological affective reaction which, like anxiety, becomes abnormal when it occurs in inappropriate circumstances, when it persists for an undue length of time, and when the child is unable to make a developmentally appropriate reaction to it." They also revise the theory of the loss of the desired love-object: "While what is lost may be an object, it may equally well be the loss of a previous state of the self. Indeed we would place emphasis on the latter rather than on the fact of the object-loss per se. When a love-object is lost, what is really lost, we believe, is the state of well-being implicit, both psychologically and biologically, in the relationship with the object. The young infant who suffers physical and psychological deprivation in the phase before object-representations have been adequately structured may show a depressive response to the loss of psychophysical well-being. Even an older child, who can distinguish adequately between self and object-representation, may react with depression to the birth of a sibling; a reaction which is not in our view an object-loss but rather a feeling of having been deprived of an ideal state, the vehicle of which was the sole possession of the mother . . . if his response is characterized by a feeling of helplessness, and shows a passive resignation in his behavior, we can consider him to be depressed." Sandler and Joffe[32] emphasize that the effect of object-loss will be greater than the loss of the state of well-being embodied in the relationship to the object-loss, as the child grows older. They define depression, in brief, as ". . . a state of helpless resignation in the face of pain, together with an inhibition both of drive discharge and ego function." They note that not all children will react in the same way to the feeling of helplessness. Some will remain fixated at their developmental level, or even regress to more immature levels, while others will make strenuous efforts to regain the former state of well-being, and as a result may react with anger and aggression during this attempt.

This work of Sandler and Joffe,[32] emphasizing that depression is a reaction to loss (either of an object or a state of well-being) with a feeling of diminished self-esteem and helplessness, enables us to understand how depressions are manifested in different ways at various levels of development. We must always bear in mind that the effect of any object-loss depends not only on the developmental stage at which such a loss occurs but also upon the individual's tolerance to pain and discomfort. As a general rule, the younger the child when the loss occurs the more serious will be the effects. Infants may remain fixated at their level of development, or regress and perhaps even die. The lack of ego development will at times impede intellectual growth. It will also interfere with the child's capacity to form adequate object relationships. The child's ability to identify with significant figures in his life may be adversely affected, and this difficulty will deleteriously affect the development of the ego-ideal, the superego, and in fact the whole personality structure. If the loss occurs during the latency years or early adolescence, most youngsters will react with open hostility and anger toward the individual who he feels has deserted and betrayed him. This inevitably leads to serious acting out and delinquency. Such defensive operations may temporarily insulate the child against his painful feelings of helplessness, but they seldom prove successful in the long run. On the contrary, they lead only to further conflict with the parents, who are likely to become increasingly hostile toward the child because of his behavior. As a result the parents become less available to the child, who still urgently needs their love and support. Many children will blame themselves for the loss they have experienced, believing that they are unacceptable, bad, and evil. This may well inhibit the expression of anger toward the parents but at the price of turning such anger against themselves. The end result will be an impoverished self-image, producing the acting out so common in depressed children. The acting-out behavior will of necessity reinforce the child's impaired self-image, further diminish his self-esteem, and serve only to increase his feelings of helplessness and depression.

The resolution of the Oedipus complex with the resultant sense of loss of the parent is an additional factor in the formation of depression in adolescents. Such a sense of loss becomes exacerbated when the child leaves for the first time for boarding school, college, or military service. Many adolescents at this age still need a parent or parent substitute to whom he can relate. Others are able to replace their parents by relating closely to their own peer group in fraternities, communes, etc. Those youngsters who are unable to accomplish this will often succumb to serious depression.

Suicide

Many physicians have failed to recognize that suicide and suicidal attempts are not infrequently encountered with children and adolescents. This may be due to the belief that adolescents and children do not become depressed and therefore are unlikely to commit suicide. Actually the rate of suicide among adolescents has shown the greatest rise of any age group. As Jacobziner[20] has emphasized: "Suicide in adolescence has increased and is assuming proportionally greater importance as deaths from other causes decline." Suicide is the fourth leading cause of death in the fourteen to nineteen-year-old age group, being surpassed only by accidents, malignancies, and homicides. It is well to bear in mind that figures for reported suicides are significantly under-reported, especially for children and adolescents. The Suicide Prevention Center of Los Angeles has estimated that half of all suicides may be disguised as accidents. We are only just becoming aware of how often accidents are subconscious attempts at self-destruction.

All statistics indicate that males outnumber females in deaths by suicide. This holds true for all ages throughout the world. Suicide attempts, however, show a reverse ratio, with females outnumbering males at every age. Toolan's[38] study of adolescent suicide at Bellevue Hospital showed a preponderance of females to males of seven to one. It is impossible, of course, to obtain accurate figures for suicide attempts, but Jacobziner[20] has estimated the ratio of attempted suicide to actual suicide at one-hundred to one.

The number of studies of suicidal attempts by children and adolescents remains low. In 1937 Bender and Schilder[7] described 18 children under eighteen years of age who either threatened or attempted suicide. These children were described as reacting to intolerable situations which made them feel unloved, leading to anger and guilt for harboring such feelings. Balser and Masterson[5] reported that in a group of 500 adolescent patients, 37 had attempted suicide. Toolan[38] reported that during the year 1960, 102 out of a total of 900 admissions to the children's and adolescent's units at Bellevue Hospital were for suicide threats and attempts. Eighteen of these children were under twelve years of age. The youngest was a five-year-old boy who attempted suicide on several occasions by burning himself on a gas heater and by pouring scalding water over himself. The author states that most of these patients came from broken and chaotic homes. Fewer than $\frac{1}{3}$ resided with both parents, and fathers were noticeably absent from the homes. These youngsters were described as immature and impulsive, and as reacting excessively to stress, even when that stress was of a minor nature. The majority were diagnosed as having behavior and character disorders. Toolan[38] divided his patients into 5 groups, as far as dynamic factors were concerned: 1) Those who were angry at another person, usually the parent or parent substitute, and where the anger was internalized in the form of guilt and depression; 2) Those who were attempting to manipulate another person, either to punish them or to gain affection and attention. These attempts were usually directed against the parents, with the accompanying fantasy of, "You will be sorry when I am dead. You will realize how badly you treated me;" 3) Youngsters who used a suicidal gesture as a signal of distress to call attention to their problems; 4) Those reacting to feelings of inner disintegration, such as hallucinatory commands; 5) Those desiring to join dead relatives.

Schrut[33] reported on 19 adolescents who attempted suicide. His group was similar to that described by Toolan,[38] and their behavior was characterized as hostile and self-destructive. Schrut[33] theorized that the child felt rejected and therefore was angry with his parents, which caused the parents in turn to become angry with the child, thereby establishing a destructive cycle.

To adequately evaluate the suicide potential is a difficult task. This is especially true for children and adolescents. For example, one may examine a teen-ager who has just made a serious suicide attempt and discover that he appears angry, rather than depressed as one might expect. All suicidal attempts, even those of a minor nature, should have a thorough psychiatric evaluation if at all possible. A period of observation in a hospital is often a great help. Such youngsters can usually be cared for on a pediatric service in a general hospital. This period of hospitalization not only protects the child from further self-destructive behavior but allows for an evaluation of the child in a neutral setting. It may also help the parents recognize the seriousness of the situation. It is not unusual to find parents reacting with anger to suicide attempts on the part of the child. They may feel disgraced or be disturbed by the personal distress the child has caused them. It is therefore necessary to involve the parents in a therapy program if the child is to return home.

Conclusion

An overview of the literature on depression in children and adolescents reveals controversy as to whether children under twelve years of age may become depressed. The author concludes that they do so, but the clinical picture differs considerably from that seen in adult depressives. From mid-adolescence on, we may expect to see a clinical pattern similar to adult depression. A theoretical explanation, emphasizing maturational changes, is offered for the development of depression in children and adolescents.

BIBLIOGRAPHY

1. Abraham, K.: Notes on the psychoanalytic investigation and treatment of manic-depressive insanity and allied conditions. In *Selected Papers.* London, Hogarth, 1927.
2. Agras, S.: The relationship of school phobia to childhood depression. *Amer J Psychiat, 116:*533-536, 1959.

3. American Handbook of Psychiatry. Volume II. New York, Basic Books, 1959.
4. Anthony, J. and Scott, P.: Manic-Depressive psychosis in childhood. *J Child Psychol Psychiat, 1:*53-72, 1960.
5. Balser, B. and Masterson, J.: Suicide in adolescents. *Amer J Psychiat, 115:*400-405, 1959.
6. Beck, A.T.: *Depression.* New York, Hoeber, 1967.
7. Bender, L. and Schilder, P.: Suicidal occupations and attempts in children. *Amer J Orthopsychiat, 7:*225-234, 1937.
8. Bibring, E.: The Mechanism of Depression. In Greenacre, P., (Ed.), *Affective Disorders.* New York, International Universities Press, 1953.
9. Bierman, J.; Silverstein, A., and Finesinger, J.: A Depression in a Six-Year-Old Boy with Acute Poliomyelitis. In *The Psychoanalytic Study of the Child, 13:*430-450. New York, International Universities Press, 1958.
10. Boulanger, J.B.: Depression in childhood. *Canad Psychiat Assn J, 11:* S.309-S.311, 1966.
11. Bowlby, J.: Childhood mourning and its implications for psychiatry. *Amer J Psychiat, 118:*481-498, 1960.
12. Burks, H.L. and Harrison, S.L.: Aggressive behavior as a means of avoiding depression. *Amer J Orthopsychiat, 32:*416-422, 1962.
13. Campbell, J.D.: Manic-Depressive disease in children. *JAMA, 158:*154-157, 1955.
14. Despert, J.L.: Suicide and depression in children. *Nervous Child, 9:*378-389, 1952.
15. Engel, G.L., and Reichsman, F.: Spontaneous and experimentally induced depressions in an infant with a Gastric Fistula. *J. Amer Psychoanal Assn, 4:*428-453, 1956.
16. Freud, S.: *Mourning and Melancholia.* Standard Edition 14. London, Hogarth Press, 1917.
17. Goldfarb, W.: Effects of psychological deprivation in infancy and subsequent stimulation. *Amer J Psychiat, 102:*18-33, 1946.
18. Harrington, M. and Hassan, J.: Depression in girls during latency. *Brit J Med Psychol, 31:*43-50, 1958.
19. Hill, O.W.: The association of childhood bereavement with suicidal attempts in depressive illness. *Brit J Psychiat, 115:*301-304, 1969.
20. Jacobziner, H.: Attempted Suicides in Adolescence. *JAMA, 191:*101-105, 1965.
21. Kanner, L.: *Child Psychiatry.* Fourth edition. Springfield, Thomas, 1972.
22. Kasanin, J. and Kaufman, M.R.: A study of the functional psychoses in childhood. *Amer J Psychiat, 9:*307-384, 1929.
23. Kaufman, I. and Heims, L.: The body image of the juvenile delinquent. *Amer J Orthopsychiat, 28:*146-159, 1958.

24. Keeler, W.R.: Children's reaction to the death of a parent. In Hoch, P. and Zubin, J., (Ed.): *Depression*. New York, Grune and Stratton, 1954.

25. Klein, M.: A contribution to the psychogenesis of Manic-Depressive states. In *Contributions to Psychoanalysis*. London, Hogarth, 1948.

26. Klerman, G.L.: Clinical research in depression. *Arch Gen Psychiat, 24:* 305-319, 1971.

27. Lehmann, H.E.: Psychiatric concepts of depression: nomenclative and classification. *Canad Psychiat Ass J, Sup. 4:*S1-S12, 1959.

28. Ling, W.; Oftedal, G. and Weinberg, W.: Depressive illness in childhood presenting as a severe headache. *Amer J Dis Child, 120:*122-124, 1970.

29. Nicoli, A.M.: Harvard dropouts: some psychiatric findings. *Amer J Psychiat, 124:*105-112, 1967.

30. Rie, H.E.: Depression in childhood—a survey of some pertinent contributions. *J Amer Acad Child Psychiat, 5:*653-685, 1967.

31. Rochlin, G.: The loss complex. *J Amer Psychoanal Ass, 7:*299-316, 1959.

32. Sandler, J. and Joffe, W.G.: Notes on childhood depression. *Int J Psychoanal, 46:*88-96, 1965.

33. Schrut, A.: Suicidal adolescents and children. *JAMA, 188:*1103-1107, 1964.

34. Sperling, M.: Equivalents of depression in children. *J Hillside Hosp, 8:* 138-148, 1959.

35. Spitz, R. and Wolf, K.M.: Anaclitic depression; an inquiry into the genesis of psychiatric conditions in early childhood. In *The Psychoanalytic Study of the Child*. 2:313-341. New York, International Universities Press, 1946.

36. Statten, T.: Depressive anxieties and their defences in childhood. *Canad Med Ass J, 84:*824-827, 1961.

37. Toolan, J.M.: Depression in children and adolescents. *Amer J Orthopsychiat, 32:*404-415, 1962.

38. Suicide and suicidal attempts in children and adolescents. *Amer J Psychiat, 118:*719-724, 1962.

CHAPTER 6

THE PSYCHOTIC ADOLESCENT IN THE CONTEXT OF HIS FAMILY

SAMUEL SLIPP, M.D.

THE MOST PREVALENT FORM of psychosis during adolescence is schizophrenia, therefore this paper will limit itself to this disorder. Unlike a physical illness, schizophrenia can best be understood in the context of the family, even though it is the patient that overtly demonstrates the symptomatology. Some of the family dynamics will be presented in order to provide the physician with background information which can be helpful in recognizing a pathological situation, making a diagnosis and facilitating a psychiatric referral.

I shall begin by historically reviewing some of the thinking concerning schizophrenia. In the nineteenth century, Kraepelin termed it Dementia Praecox, since it so often began during adolescence and led to mental deterioration. Bleuler[1] was one of the first psychiatrists who did not agree with this formulation, and he developed a functional point of view as opposed to the organic one held earlier. He therefore renamed the disorder schizophrenia, referring to the splitting, or lack of integration, of mental functioning. By this Bleuler referred to disorders of thought, such as blocking, in which the individual's thought and speech suddenly and unaccountably stop; and looseness of associations, in which the usual connections between sequences of thoughts are absent or obscured. In the area of feelings, he noted marked ambivalence, a condition in which the patient expressed contradictory emotions (such as love and hate) toward the same person or idea. The patient also showed flattening of his expressions of affect. In his interpersonal relations, he was found to be unresponsive, withdrawn, and easily distractible.

Currently, we do not think of schizophrenia as a discrete disease entity, but as a syndrome which occurs at various ages, has different behavioral patterns, prognoses, and probable etiologies. The one common factor appears to be the functional adaptation of the patient at an infantile level of mental functioning, which Freud termed the primary process. The patient's language appears bizarre and detached from reality, since he uses the type of thought occurring in infancy and in dreams. This is self-centered, grandiose, and employs wishful thinking. He may not differentiate himself from others, between others, or may even consider opposites as if they were the same. Even his own thoughts and feelings may not be distinguished from others. For example, he may attribute his own unacceptable thoughts and feelings to others (projection) or be overly influenced by those of others (introjection). He may state he is someone else, or that he can read other's thoughts and they his.

Adolescent schizophrenia can be divided into two broad categories. The first is the chronic or process type, which appears earlier in life. It is less related to interpersonal trauma and more to genetic, prenatal, and organic factors. It begins in infancy or childhood, continues with exacerbations and remissions into adolescence, and generally has a poorer prognosis. The second is the acute, reactive type which begins during adolescence and seems more related to familial and socio-psychological factors. It is characterized by a sudden onset, runs a florid though briefer course, and has a high rate of remission.

The chronic or process type of schizophrenia, which appears more related to organic factors, will be discussed first. The earliest form is infantile autism, a condition in which the child is emotionally detached from birth and is unable to establish relationships with people. Follow-up studies of recovered autistic children by Eisenberg and Kanner[3,4] show that they remain self-centered, continue to show social unawareness, and have difficulty relating. Another group of children develop a psychosis later, between 2 and 4 years of age, which Mahler[5] has termed the Symbiotic Syndrome. These children remain excessively tied to their mothers, since they are unable to mentally internalize the mother and to function separately. Clinically they demonstrate a low frustration tolerance, temper tantrums, tenuous relations with people, poor judgment, and multiple neurotic symptoms. Some of these children do not become overtly psychotic until adolescence. The third group develops childhood schizophrenia before the age of 11. A very high percentage of childhood schizophrenia is later diagnosed as adolescent or adult schizophrenia.[6]

The impact of any innately abnormal child upon its parents is enormous. The intense guilt, shame, and loss of self esteem by the parents may result in either rejection or infantilizing overprotection of the child. For example, the mother may devote most of her time to the abnormal child while neglecting the rest of the family. In other cases, both parents may protect their own self esteem by rejecting the child and blaming the other parent (or the other's side of the family) for the disorder. The parental conflict that develops from these methods of dealing with the guilt may be so intense as to threaten the stability of the marriage. Not only does the child need psychiatric help, but the parents need help in coping with their own conflicted feelings. They need to ventilate their feelings, and be reassured that no one is to blame. The guidance and support that the physician can offer the parents can be crucial in enabling them to deal with their feelings toward each other as well as toward the child.

The second type of schizophrenia is the acute, reactive form. A good deal of research indicates that there is a strong correlation between family interaction and this form of schizophrenia. The main factor appears to be that the parents unintentionally prevent the adolescent from developing as a separate, autonomous individual. He is not responded to as a unique individual; instead the parents need the child to work out their own emotional problems.[7] Thus the child becomes enmeshed in a family pattern of interaction in which he feels responsible for the self esteem and mental health of his parents. The psychosis manifests itself during adolescence when this pattern comes into conflict with the adolescent's need to emancipate himself from the family.

The following case of a young man, who had an overt paranoid psychotic break with grandiose delusions, demonstrates a typical pattern of family interaction. His parents only accepted him when he fulfilled their survival needs as individuals and as a family. They demanded that he behave in a rigidly prescribed manner in order to make *them* feel important and adequate. Anything that he did which was competitive with them or did not live up to their expectations threatened their own sense of worth. In addition, the patient had been placed into the role of peacemaker whenever his parents had a disagreement. Thus his parents made him feel responsible for keeping their marriage together. As a youngster, he had behaved as a *model child,* always submitting to his parents' wishes concerning how he should think, feel, and behave. However, always complying with their demands left him constricted and alienated from his own feelings, thoughts, and judgment. Separation from his parents was experienced with a dread of dying, since he felt he could not survive without them.

The responsibility the patient felt for the self esteem and mental health of his parents reinforced the self centered, grandiose type of thinking normally found in childhood. He felt his own feelings, thoughts, and behavior determined the fate of his parents. Thus feelings and thoughts were not differentiated from action. To be angry meant to destroy or be destroyed; while to disrupt their relationship meant that he or his parents would lose their sense of worth and not survive intact.

Freud first described this self-centered type of thinking and termed it narcissism. It was later experimentally studied by the Swiss psychologist Piaget.[8] To the infant, objects are felt to come and go as a function of his own actions, as if they were not separate, but that there was a magical cause and effect relationship. In this family, as well as in other families I have clinically observed, each person's self esteem and psychological survival was felt to be dependent upon the other's behavior. I term this the *symbiotic survival pattern.* Because there is no distinct cleavage developed between one's self and others, nor between one's subjective feelings (fantasies, wishful thinking, etc.) and external reality, the symbiotic survival pattern appears to reinforce primary process thinking.

Separation from these families is equated unconsciously with worthlessness, loss of identity, abandonment, helplessness, and psychological death. Each feels controlled by his overwhelming sense of responsibility for the other's survival, who is also seen as helpless and vulnerable. Adaptation to these families makes separation fraught with guilt, as well as being maladaptive to functioning in the outside world. Frequently these families are socially isolated, and they project their problems onto outsiders, thereby instilling distrust. Family members often feel passive and controlled, and do not feel competent to master their environment, which is perceived as hostile and threatening.

In general for families with this type of interaction, the parents themselves have not individuated during their own adolescence, having rigidly conformed to their families of origin. Self-assertion was unacceptable, and they were unable to accept and integrate their own feelings. They often seek the continuation of a parental figure to assume responsibility and to control them in order to feel loved and important. They were not trained for independent existence. Frequently the parents are still pathologically dependent upon and dominated by their own parents, or each parent may manipulate his spouse or a child into acting out a parental role in the family. When a spouse assumes a parental function to his or her partner, the family may tend to use a child as a scapegoat upon whom to project blame. The child thus serves as a vehicle for the expression of anger and frustration which would be too threatening to the pathological dependency if dealt with directly, that is, between the parents. In the symbiotic survival pattern there is a sharing of ego functions, as if the family members were merged into one person. There is too much togetherness, and separateness is denied. To sustain the appearance of family solidarity, each individual's needs cannot be acknowledged or gratified. In effect, this isolates each member and prevents true intimacy and sharing from evolving. Since separateness is too threatening, differences need to be denied. Thus disagreements and conflict may not be acknowledged openly nor resolved. Wynne[9] has noted that many of these families erect a facade of being a happy, normal family since they deny problems so massively. He has used the term "pseudomutuality" to describe this process. Other families are in a state of perpetual conflict which never gets resolved. One point that needs to be emphasized is that the parents do not maliciously wish to harm their children. They are unable to function otherwise, since they are themselves so enmeshed in the symbiotic survival pattern.

To achieve autonomy under normal circumstances, the adolescent must have experienced parenting which respected him as an individual, provided appropriate guidance, and encouraged self reliance and trust in himself and others. His parents had to be responsive to him so that he could grow up in touch with his feelings, thoughts, wishes, and abilities. Only in this way would he be able to integrate thoughts and feelings and to work out the inner controls and the standards necessary for normal functioning. If successful, the adolescent learns to trust his judgment and to have confidence in his decision-making, which is so important a part of this period. His self esteem and perception are less vulnerable to the criticism of others, since he has evolved a relatively stable identity with an adequate sense of who he is. However, if the adolescent is enmeshed in the symbiotic survival pattern, the family relationship is so engulfing, stifling, and confining that he may retreat into a world of fantasy to sustain any sense of himself. Separation from the family is not only fraught with ambivalence and guilt, but is disruptive to his personality, since he has evolved only an *as if* personality and not a solid identity.

What can the physician look for when parents bring their adolescent to him with concerns about his lack of drive, poor school performance, day dreaming, social isolation, or his changed behavior toward them? Unless the patient is floridly psychotic, diagnosis is often difficult, since a certain amount of withdrawal or instability occurs normally during adolescence. However, a variety of behavior patterns can alert the physician to the possibility of a latent or incipient schizophrenia.

One such pattern is represented by the schizoid adolescent who is usually socially isolated, excessively shy, secretive, and relates poorly. When he talks to you, he has poor eye contact. He may speak in a monotone, have flat facies, and may appear younger than his age. An example, mentioned previously, is the *model child* who is overly compliant and well behaved. Even though he presents himself as essentially normal, he does not come across as a real person to whom you can respond emotionally. A quality of aloofness, vagueness, and uninvolvement creates an impenetrable barrier. He shows shallow or flat affect and has an overly intellectualized and mechanistic way of thinking. For example, he may think in terms of superficial stereotypes, putting people into categories, and making unwarranted assumptions. Another form of premorbid personality is the stormy, emotionally unstable type, who shows intense mood swings, temper tantrums, is overly sensitive, and has poor judgment. Pseudopsychopathic behavior may be demonstrated by some latent schizophrenics, characterized by stealing, truancy, or suicidal or homicidal thoughts. Another variety is the pseudo-neurotic, who shows multiple neurotic symptoms, particularly obsessions, phobias, hypochondriasis, and depression. They may be unable to concentrate, be overly intellectualized, obsessively concerned with religious, mystical, or philosophical issues, think in rigid categories, and substitute day dreaming for interpersonal relations. Another subtype is the pseudo-defective, who functions at a retarded intellectual level.

The onset of frank psychosis during adolescence is ushered in by a sudden and marked change in behavior. Such patients may neglect their body care or clothing, and become excessively preoccupied with bodily functions. They may make bizarre statements particularly about their secondary sexual characteristics or their sexual organs. They may engage in repetitive rituals, such as handwashing. They may lose their outside goals and interests resulting in failure at school and social isolation from their peers. On examination, the adolescent may appear vague, staring vacantly into space, grimacing (perhaps in response to hallucinations), or displaying uncontrolled body movements. His speech may not flow freely and his thinking may contain gaps or be so loosely connected as to be unintelligible. He may also be very difficult to understand due to his use of cryptic, highly personalized symbolic speech. More obvious symptoms are overt delusions of a grandiose or persecutory nature. He may state he is a famous political or religious figure, for example, or feel that the F.B.I. or some other group are spying on him. He may feel that people are looking at him or talking about him (ideas of reference), or that he is being controlled by an electronic device or machine. He may state that others can read his mind or that he can read their mind and know what they are thinking. Visual or auditory hallucinations may be present, or he may go into a state of catatonic excitement or stupor. Although bizarre dress and preoccupation with mysticism and the occult were once considered reliable indicators, this has to be evaluated in the context of their natural occurrence in the current adolescent culture. From clinical experience, I have noted that multiple, superficial, self inflicted scratches on the wrists, forearms, face, or thighs are often part of the picture of a psychotic decompensation.

A careful medical workup is essential for the overtly psychotic adolescent. He should be questioned about drug use, since diet pills, amphetamines, L.S.D., mescaline, marihuana, cocaine, etc. may simulate a paranoid schizophrenia. Familiarity with the language of the drug scene or involvement with other youngsters who are known drug users may be a clue to his taking drugs. However, one must keep in mind that seriously disturbed and prepsychotic adolescents may also use drugs. The drugs may undermine the defenses of the youngsters and precipitate a latent schizophrenia into an overt psychotic reaction. Other diagnoses that must be ruled out are epilepsy, endocrine dysfunctions, infections, blood dyscrasias, encephalitis, subdural hematoma, and brain tumor.

Ability to establish rapport with the physician, to be emotionally responsive, and to initiate conversation militate against psychosis as the diagnosis. If he is functioning well in other areas of his life, is involved in a normal peer group, and if his parents seem to be reasonably well adjusted, warm, and relate well, then the likelihood is that any current symptoms are transitory. The parents need to be reassured that this is probably part of the normal process of emancipation. A useful book that can be recommended is aptly entitled, "Patience and Fortitude, The Parents' Guide to Adolescence," by Graham B. Blaine, Jr. Even under the best of circumstances, the separation and emancipation of a child is a difficult process for parents. The disruption of any long standing relationship of intimacy may normally result in depression and mourning.

The sympathetic physician can help the parents work through their feelings of hurt, loss, and emptiness at seeing their child leave the nest. He needs to reassure them that their effectiveness as good parents is not at issue, emphasizing the positive aspects of their concern, but pointing out that it is perfectly normal for the child to create distance from them in order to break his dependency. By establishing new relationships with outsiders, he is consolidating his identity as a person. The physician can then encourage the parents to be patient and to enrich their lives in other ways.

A very real clue to the seriousness of the adolescent's pathology can be obtained from close scrutiny of the family interaction while they are in the office. Family members may not seem responsive to each other. When one member brings up a topic, the other member may interrupt or change it repeatedly and discuss another matter. Thus there does not appear to be a dialogue, but a series of unconnected monologues. Even within the monologue, there may be unrelated shifts in topics or focus of attention. Often disagreements or differences between family members does not come out in the open but are avoided or denied. Some families seem to be in a perpetual state of uproar, with constant interruptions, yelling, and unresolved conflict. Each member seems to be preoccupied with his own needs, viewpoint, and thoughts. The parents may also repeatedly interrupt the adolescent when he is speaking, answering for him and assuming to know his feelings and thoughts. As a general rule, if the parents seem intrusive and disregard his integrity as an individual, it compounds the seriousness of the presenting problem. The physician's own feelings can be extremely helpful diagnostically. If he empathically experiences a strange vagueness or emptiness with the adolescent, or if he finds himself feeling frustrated, confused, and annoyed with the parents' excessive control and manipulation, he is likely to be dealing with a serious situation. None of these findings are sufficient in themselves, and are only significant when integrated with the rest of the picture. If, from the history, the adolescent appears enmeshed in such a symbiotic survival pattern, a psychiatric referral is essential.

How the referral is made often determines whether psychiatric treatment will be accepted or not. Some parents feel quite threatened by the thought of psychiatrists probing their secrets, and may want to focus all attention on the adolescent as if only he were the problem. They may wish to deny their own involvement and want the physician or psychiatrist to take total responsibility for changing or controlling the youngster. Some of our research at the Family Therapy Unit of the New York University— Bellevue Medical Center indicates that it is commonly the father who feels most threatened. Involving him may be a prerequisite to successful psychotherapy. The physician should not fall into a sympathetic alliance with the youngster and be cool, withholding, or rejecting of the parents. This may only reinforce their guilt, and by alienating them, lead to their sabotaging treatment. On the other hand, the physician should not fall into an alliance or form a secret pact with the parents against the youngster. The adolescent should never be tricked into a psychiatric referral, since this only increases his distrust and resistance to treatment. The physician needs to help the parents become aware that everyone in a family affects one another. In order to treat the adolescent's problems more effectively therefore, the psychiatrist may wish to see other members of the family besides the patient. The psychiatrist's job is not to be judgmental. He is not concerned with affixing blame, but with helping them improve their interpersonal relationships. The parents' and the patient's anxieties and expectations of psychotherapy should be explored openly so that they can get a clearer picture of what will happen when they visit the psychiatrist. The physician must be aware of and take into account the parents' defensiveness due to their sense of failure and guilt over their child's illness. As an added bit of information, I find using the term schizophrenia with the family to be deleterious. It tends to provoke terror and still implies a hopeless prognosis. The term nervous breakdown is less emotionally loaded, yet does not minimize the seriousness of the problem.

The majority of disturbed adolescents receiving treatment can be maintained at home, especially if the parents are also involved in the treatment. Although not limited to adolescents, 84 percent of acutely disturbed patients referred for hospitalization at the Colorado Psychopathic Hospital[10] were able to be treated as outpatients when the families were involved in treatment. Other studies also show that outpatient care, when properly handled, can avert hospitalization and give even more promising followup results. However, when optimal circumstances are not available, hospitalization may be the only alternative. For the acute adolescent schizophrenic reaction this is usually brief. If the adolescent is overtly psychotic and agitated, immediate referral is essential, since he may attempt suicide, become assaultive, run away, or behave irrationally with his friends. Embarrassment may make it difficult for him to face them later when he has recovered.

In summary, if in doubt it is important to obtain a psychiatric consultation. Medication alone, without working out the patient's and the family's problems, can only provide temporary symptomatic relief. In many places, family therapy or concurrent therapy with the parents may not be available, and the psychiatrist may have to concentrate his efforts on the adolescent. In such cases, and because of his ongoing relationship, the nonpsychiatric physician may be in a good position to provide support to the parents. By seeing the parents regularly and actively collaborating with the psychiatrist, the physician may not only help the parents, but may facilitate the adolescent's progress as well.

BIBLIOGRAPHY

1. Bleuler, E.: Dementia Praecox or the Group of Schizophrenias. International Univ., New York, 1952.
2. Freud, S.: The Interpretation of Dreams, Hogarth Press, London, 1953.
3. Eisenberg, L.: Autistic child in adolescence. *Am J Psychiatry, 112*:607-612, 1956.
4. Eisenberg, L. and Kanner, L.: Early infantile autism 1943-1955. *Am J Orthopsychiat, 26*:556-566, 1956.
5. Mahler, M.S.: Severe emotional disturbances in childhood: psychosis. In Arieti, S. (Ed.) American Handbook of Psychiatry, Vol. 1, Basic Books, New York, pp. 816-839, 1959.
6. Freedman, A.M. and Bender, L.: When the childhood schizophrenic grows up. *Am J Orthopsychiat, 27*:553-565, 1957.

7. Lidz, T.; Fleck, S. and Cornelison, A.R.: Marital schism and marital skew. In Schizophrenia and the Family. International Universities Press, New York, pp. 133-146, 1965.

8. Piaget, J.: Realism and the origin of the idea of participation. In The Child's Conception of the World. Littlefield, Adams, Patterson, N.J., pp. 123-168, 1963.

9. Wynne, L.C.; Ryckoff, I.M.; Day, J. and Hirsch, S.I.: Pseudomutuality in the family relations of schizophrenics, *Psychiatry, 21:*205-220, 1958.

10. Pittman, F.S.; DeYoung, C.; Flomenhaft, K.; Kaplan, D.M. and Langsley, D.G.: Crisis Family Therapy. In Masserman, J. (Ed.), Current Psychiatric Therapies. Vol. 6, Grune and Stratton, New York, 1966.

CHAPTER 7

CHANGING PATTERNS OF
SEXUALITY IN ADOLESCENCE

ALEXANDRA SYMONDS, M.D.

IN RECENT YEARS we have all observed very distinct changes in the sexual attitudes and sexual values of young people in our culture. These changes are mainly in the area of increased freedom in sexual activities, at a younger age, and with less feelings of guilt. This is especially true for girls, and especially for girls of middle and upper classes. One recent study showed that 10 years ago 27 percent of young men had had their first sexual experience with prostitutes, while today the figure is approximately 2 percent. Not only has the incidence of intercourse of youngsters increased, but their social patterns have changed. They no longer hide their behavior from their elders. We now see boys and girls engaging in close bodily contact, fondling, kissing clinging together more openly, with relatively little guilt or shame.

In this paper I will discuss the most frequent problems involving sex and the adolescent which have come to my attention in my practice. Before discussing the clinical situations I will go into certain factors which have laid the groundwork for our attitudes and problems today.

While we have a tendency to condemn the behavior of youngsters today, we forget what has made this behavior possible. In the last 50 years there have been major changes in the basic patterns of family life, religious life and daily community life of the entire world. We have gradually moved away from the absolute authority of the father in the family. Women have been allowed to participate more and more outside the home. We have come to realize that the Victorian attitudes towards sex were excessively prudish, often causing exaggerated guilt and depression over normal thoughts and impulses. Fear of sex was unhealthy and caused much anguish, as well as many psychiatric disturbances. As a result of these excessively repressive attitudes, many parents in the last two generations were determined to spare their children some of their own personal suffering in groping for sexual adjustment, and they tried to create an atmosphere in which sex could be seen as a more natural and wholesome part of life and of love. Let us keep this in mind before we automatically condemn the youngsters of today. We adults have prepared the way for what is happening, with the best of intentions, and we are now left with some unexpected and undesirable complications.

Another important factor is that in the last 25 years the world atmosphere has been one of increasing hostility, almost constant involvement in war, and hanging over our heads, an awareness that the atom bomb could wipe out mankind. This atmosphere has had a distinct effect on our young people. It has increased the usual generation gap. It has increased the usual fear and uncertainty of adolescent searching. Today's youngsters have become the *Love Generation.* "Make love not war" is their slogan. A few years ago some teenagers were calling themselves *flower children.* Young runaways are taken into group pads where they receive comfort and shelter from other teenagers. In times of mass anxiety people cling to each other for support. In London during the blitz, the usual reserve of the Englishman broke down. Together they shared the shelters and the hardships. Today we see this happening in our young people. They seek each other out more than ever for support. And along with this, they are having more physical contact. A large part of the sexual activities of youngsters is not adult genital sex, but a primitive huddling together for simple body contact. Many adolescents go through the motions of sex, without love, or other feeling, but in an impersonal way merely as an attempt to break through their sense of isolation, and make contact with another human being.

The third condition of interest in discussing adolescent sex is the fact that while youngsters are given more freedoms today, have more money, have greater leeway to make their own choices and their own decisions, they are not more mature than in former years. If anything, teenagers are more dependent than ever. Parents support young married couples through college and further. Some parents support young unmarried couples, even when they are not in favor of the relationship. Prior to this generation premarital sex was illicit and privately worked out, as part of the separation from home. While today it often goes on within the dependent relationship of child and parent.

I have frequently seen in my clinical practice that the parents are deliberately brought into their youngster's sex life in order to prolong the dependent relationship. Some adolescents fear the maturation process. They feel emotionally unprepared to be on their own and therefore they create a hostile dependency on their parents. This happens in homes where the parents have been excessively intrusive, overprotective or infantilizing. Many crises result in adolescence as a result of these factors, and they may center around sexual behavior. For example, one mother came to me in panic because she found a letter addressed to her 15-year old daughter from a boy, discussing intimate sex. She told me that this letter was left opened, on her daughter's desk. "She must have known I would read it." Another girl invited her boyfriend to spend the night in her home, and then slipped into his room in such a way that her parents could hear. In both instances, a crisis was precipitated in which the parents sought help. It did not take much questioning of the girls to find that they wanted their parents to know about their activities but could not tell them directly. This type of maneuver is often an attempt on the part of a youngster to have their parents set limits for them because they cannot handle it themselves.

In some families, parents discuss sex too freely with their children. They may go around the house in the nude, or even discuss their own sex life with their children. This is sexually stimulating to a child, and causes a confused, anxious and precocious sexuality in the adolescent. Some of the most disturbed adolescents I have seen are products of excessively permissive hippie parents who have allowed their children to view the sex act at an extremely young age under the mistaken idea that privacy, modesty and clothing are merely evidences of "uptight" establishment attitudes. In their attempt to "go back to "nature" they often cause their youngsters excessive anxiety due to the constant sexual stimulation which they are precociously exposed to. These are the youngsters who are likely to participate in impersonal and excessive sex, such as the type in group pads. Their own sexual boundaries and sexual identity is not clearcut since in their childhood there were no hard and fast separations between parent and child.

What sort of clinical problems result from these conditions? By far the most common questions directed at me by parents, teenagers, teachers, social workers and others who work with youth are: How far is it healthy for a young girl to go in her sexual activities? Should we prescribe or encourage the "pill," or other contraception?" Each situation must be evaluated separately to try to determine the emotional climate in which the girl is at the time. Remember that today's adolescents are not necessarily more mature emotionally or physiologically, they merely have less guilt about their sexual impulses and desires, and have more opportunity to gratify them. We therefore have a paradoxical situation in which a youngster may feel a certain social pressure to have more freedom in sex than he or she is ready for. Most teenage girls are still fearful of their first sexual experience and have many conflicts involving pleasing their boyfriend by going along with his urging. When a girl is in conflict, I encourage her to take very seriously her own doubts and hesitations, and to avoid situations which ultimately lead to self-hate and depression. I have found that too early involvement in sex is a sign of low self-esteem and depression in a young girl. This type of girl becomes involved in a shallow, desperate kind of sexual promiscuity in her attempt to relieve her despair. Unfortunately, it only accentuates her depression rather than relieving it, since she invariably hates herself for her behavior. It is often possible to help an immature youngster not to have sexual relations when she is not really ready for it. One patient of 16 was upset because she found that she was very affectionate while walking with her boyfriend on the street, but when they were alone together, she froze up. She thought she was frigid. It turned out that they were alone, sort of, in the boy's room, with his whole family at home. As we discussed this she realized that this was inappropriate and not what she wanted. In several cases it has been possible to head off an orgy of promiscuity in a depressed young girl by giving her an opportunity to explore her feelings. A sympathetic adult, such as a physician, can be of great help. A judgmental attitude is sure to increase depression and self-destructive behavior, whereas interest and respect can be the turning point for such a patient. Adolescents are looking for adults who can help them place sensible boundaries on their behavior.

Most of the time the physician is not consulted until the question of contraception comes up. By this time the adolescent has already had sexual relations or is determined to have them. Here we are faced with a revolution in psychological dynamics. Now, it is the female who is called upon to take the initiative in her sexual behavior. Until recent years when a young girl was being wooed by a young man, she could place her trust in him that he would avoid a pregnancy. He was the strong, dependable person who would look after her if they actually came to have intercourse. He was as concerned as she. He had to exercise self-control over his sexual impulses. Today, a girl must now step out of her role of compliance and dependency, the traditionally female role. She must take precautions for herself. She must arrange far in advance for her sexual life. In marriage this is understandable, but before marriage this causes many complications. Youngsters are called upon to develop a pseudomaturity in their sex life and many cannot do it. I believe that this is one important reason why illegitimate births are on the rise, despite the increased efficiency and availability of birth control methods. A young 18-year-old girl I am treating has had three potential pregnancies in the last year and a half. On three occasions she has made what she called *mistakes* in taking the birth control pill. However, these were not simple errors or lapses of memory. They were indications that she could not relinquish her deep-seated dependency; taking the pill required a certain amount of healthy self interest which was not always possible for her.

If a youngster reaches the point where she requests the birth control pill—I feel that she should have it, even if her parents are not aware of it. It is important for the family physician to treat this request confidentially or it can have a deleterious effect on the adolescent.

If an individual is determined to have sex, we cannot stop her, we can only help guide her to avoid serious complications. If you feel that your own ethics or moral values make this impossible, then I urge you not to violate your patient's confidence by telling her parents about the request. This does not help—it merely makes it less likely that the girl will turn to any adult in the future. What you could do, if the youngster seems to have many psychological problems, or is prematurely driven into sexual activities, is suggest that she seek help, or offer to help her (through her parents) get psychotherapy. This can be done without telling her parents the specific reason for it. Several birth control clinics in New York City changed their policy in 1968 making it possible to give contraceptives to adolescents who are minors and who have never been pregnant. They found increasing pressure for this service from young teen-agers and now openly dispense their services to this group. 15 percent of their new patients are now under 18 and unmarried. Several of these clinics run groups in which young teen-agers, both boys and girls, can discuss sex and sexual problems with informed adults. While there is no law specifically forbidding this policy in New York State, intercourse under the age of 17 is still considered statutory rape. However, to add to the confusion, a bill was passed in June of 1972 granting the right to any medical treatment without parental consent if the physician considers it an emergency. Thus, *emancipated minors* are being treated under this category.

On occasion a mother has asked me to recommend contraception to her daughter, or to discuss it with her because the mother felt awkward or conflicted about it. When the request originates with the parent and not the child I feel it is inappropriate for me to be a go-between. Discussions about sex are intimate, personal, and belong to the privacy of the mother-daughter relationship. It is far better for the mother to talk directly with her daughter about it, instead of asking someone else to do it. I know of many occasions in which a mother has directed her doctor to examine and prescribe a diaphragm or the pill, without her daughter asking for it, or even without knowing for sure whether her daughter has been involved sexually. This is generally a very hostile, manipulative mother who is oblivious or insensitive to her child's feelings. Any doctor who goes along with this is participating in a hostile invasion of the youngster's psyche, usually premature or sometimes sexually provocative. On occasion a father will be so overinvolved with his daughter's life, that he will bring up the subject. Again, this is an intrusion into the daughter's privacy, and definitely sexually stimulating albeit on an unconscious basis.

To illustrate the many psychological implications of using the *pill:* I was consulted in a situation in which a 19-year-old girl was in therapy for profound depression and self-destructive behavior. Two years earlier she had had an out-of-wedlock baby and given it up for adoption. She considered herself evil, sinful, and dirty whenever she was aware of sexual desires. On occasion, with much guilt and self-criticism, she had sexual relations, but refused to use any precautions against possible pregnancy because this would only prove how low and sinful she was. She consulted her doctor because of severe acne, and he told her that he was going to prescribe birth control pills for her skin. She left in a panic, never took them, and never went back.

I have been speaking mainly of girls. Boys, too, are being affected by the changes in sexual standards. They are perhaps suffering more than girls since they are no longer being encouraged by the adults to use sexual restraint, to develop self-discipline, and to bear the responsibility of their sexual behavior. Therefore, they tend more and more to indulge themselves in their sexual desires, without a maturing process going along with it. Now they can shift from being taken care of by their parents, to being taken care of by their girlfriends. Perhaps this is one of the factors which contributes to the phenomenon of the Uni-sex. We now see boys and girls dressing alike, looking alike, and inwardly they are often very confused about their sexual identity. I see many young boys who are excessively narcissistic in their preoccupation with appearance, who have been over-indulged by their parents, and who have very little tolerance for strenuous effort. These boys often break down early in college. Their concept of masculinity is vague and undeveloped.

In conclusion, I want to say that I am in favor of some of the changes which have occurred in sexual attitudes in recent years. Attitudes change in cycles. We were too sexually repressed 50 years ago. Now we are seeing signs of too much sexual preoccupation. Sex is not an end in itself but only a part of life. Shallow, mechanized sex leaves young people feeling hopeless and in despair. It becomes another disillusionment in adult life. The increased freedom in sexual behavior can give the illusion of greater maturity or depth in relatedness. This is obviously not so, and as adults we must keep this in mind. Many adults are rejecting youngsters because of their increased freedom in sexual behavior and they fail to recognize that underlying this behavior is a desperate search for meaning and relatedness.

CHAPTER 8

PSYCHOLOGICAL MANAGEMENT
OF ADOLESCENT DRUG ABUSE

ROBERT E. GOULD, M.D.

T HE TREATMENT OF drug abuse in adolescents is often a difficult
matter, partly because of the complexity of adolescents themselves. In considering the problem, I shall present my own approach to treatment—what I have done, what has worked and
what has not—and some thoughts as to what *ought* to be done,
for treatment to be effective. This involves ideas for projects and
treatment modalities which do not yet exist.

Because of widespread confusion in this area, it is important to
begin defining drug abuse—how it should be distinguished from
drug use—and at what point use becomes abuse. It may be
essential for determining, for example, whether or not one should
treat a drug-using youngster for whom the community is requesting treatment. Parents may call and say, "My son is on marijuana.
What am I going to do?" When I respond by asking, "How is it
hurting him? How is it interfering with his daily living?" they
exclaim, "But you don't seem to understand, he is *smoking marijuana!*" This issue is so emotionally charged, that many parents
are unable to recognize that the act of smoking pot does not in
itself constitute a problem requiring professional intervention.

It is possible to view any kind of drug intake as drug abuse.
Taking alcohol, tranquilizers, or any mood-changing drug when
not medically prescribed can be considered drug abuse. However,
such a strict definition has limited value in our drug-oriented
culture. A considerable amount of drug-taking is generally ac-

cepted (although not necessarily approved) by the dominant culture which sets standards. But when a *new* drug, such as marijuana, is introduced, generally by the youth culture, the reaction against it can be violent. Taking marijuana, then, is automatically considered drug abuse, whereas alcohol use is rationalized as almost a social necessity unless one shows signs of chronic alcoholism.

Alcohol is so accepted in this country that it is not even considered a drug in ordinary parlance. When I have asked young patients "Do you take drugs? What do you take?" they respond, "Well, pot, LSD . . ." and so on. And then I say, "How about alcohol? Have you ever tried alcohol?" "Oh, sure I've drunk alcohol, but I didn't like it." So brainwashed are the young drug takers, like older members of our culture, that they don't even include alcohol when asked to list every drug they have tried.

Practically speaking, one should consider that *drug abuse* exists when the drug intake interferes with a person's normal way of life—and in the adolescent we mean his growth and development. When he's having difficulty with peer relations, in school or in the performance of the usual tasks and everyday activities of adolescents, then he is taking drugs to the point of abuse. Under this definition much drug taking on a regular basis is eliminated. There are many students in high school and college who take marijuana on weekends, sometimes even on a nightly basis, and LSD occasionally. They often do very well in school and maintain good interpersonal relations. They may even have good relations with their parents. As I see it, this is not drug abuse. One man's drug abuse can be another man's fun and entertainment. To distinguish, we must ask, what is his background? What are the cultural norms? What kind of life is he leading? What are his goals? Is he organizing his life so as to fulfill his personal potential?

A few years ago I was roundly criticized when I stated that I thought it was healthy and normal for youngsters to experiment with marijuana and that if the adolescent knows what the effects of the drug are and realizes that physically marijuana is less harmful than alcohol and cigarettes and that psychologically it is less addicting, then there is little to keep him from experimenting.

It should not be too difficult for my generation to remember how we tried alcohol and cigarettes in our adolescence, out of curiosity or the desire to be grown up, or to do something daring or forbidden. The adolescent today, in trying marijuana, is doing very much the same thing with fewer risks. The average pot-smoker does not go on to harder drugs unless he is so vulnerable that the need for drugs as a way of life takes over. But, if this happens, then it would happen even if he never started with marijuana; it would happen starting with alcohol—because most youngsters still try alcohol before they try pot.

I shall describe two clinical examples of drug-using youngsters, seen individually, after which I wish to consider therapeutic modalities which offer more promise for the treatment of drug abusers.

The first case focuses on intrafamilial factors which, when prevalent and important, can best be handled on a one-to-one basis. When societal and cultural factors are more important, as in the second case, then the one-to-one approach may fail.

Case 1: Jerry was a 20 year old boy referred to me by his parents because he had dropped out of college, was heavily into pot and acid, did not want to work and wanted to spend all of his time on the Lower East Side or East village (the analog to the Haight-Ashbury section of San Francisco). The father had been very poor in his youth. He had to go to law school at night and had to work during the day. He became a labor lawyer dedicated to fighting for the underdog (this was at a time when the unions were the underdog) and he was helping struggling unions to get started against powerful and oppressive employers. Having begun his career at the height of the Depression, now at the age of 52, he still claimed to be acutely aware of economic and social injustices. Jerry's mother, who was fifty years old, had also been very poor in her youth and had dropped out of college to help support her younger brothers. Later she became a writer and she shared the same political and social philosophy as her husband. The father's law practice prospered. He began to represent insurance companies and the now powerful labor unions, in marked contrast to his earlier efforts for the working man.

The couple had a son, Jerry, and a daughter and moved to a fashionable New York suburb and enjoyed all the material advantages of upper-middle-class life. In this articulate home environment the children grew up hearing a great deal of the parents' liberal social views and philosophy, but the family's life-style did not match the ideals they expressed. Jerry entered therapy, not because he wanted to be cured or to change his values, but because he was desperately unhappy and at times uncontrollably angry and he knew that his drug taking was an effort to control the feelings of unhappiness, anger, emptiness and disillusionment which he could not put his finger on. He had no close relationships and several girls with whom he had sexual relations had told him that they felt that he could not be warm and he could not love. This hurt him a great deal. What emerged in therapy was a very peculiar ambivalence in Jerry's feelings towards his parents. He had identified with their ideals and with their stated beliefs. Much of this was internalized and therefore egosyntonic. Now he felt cheated and angry about the hypocrisy that he sensed in them. Their liberalism, as he saw it, consisted only in cocktail party philosophizing and in contributing money to civil rights groups such as SNCC and CORE. They did little to change the conditions of the disadvantaged. Furthermore, he believed that they felt unfullfilled in their own lives and although committed to the *good things* (i.e. material comforts) he was convinced they felt guilty about *selling out* their principles. They quarreled frequently but at several family treatment sessions it was clear that even their quarrels never touched on what was troubling them. I found that on confrontation they used rationalization, intellectualization and denial to keep from facing the fact that they were not living according to the values they were preaching. What faced their son Jerry, if he continued on the conventional path of college and professional school, was a life very much like theirs which seemed to him sterile, empty and banal. Yet undeniably, society would say that this family "had made it." Jerry had no rebuttal for their arguments about the importance of college to prepare for a good job and for all the things that would make life comfortable. Dropping out of college and gravitating to the East

Village and the hippie world actually provided Jerry with an escape from a world in which he felt stifled and trapped. At the same time he was also acting out the socialistic ideals his parents had preached but failed to practice. He lived in a commune, shared his meager goods and espoused brotherly love. Jerry in effect was gratifying several needs. Although his parents expressed strong disapproval of his behavior, Jerry covertly hoped and felt that perhaps he would win their respect for acting out a way of life that they were talking about but not living. By defecting to hippie-ism he could also express his anger, renounce what his parents had achieved and hurt them by going against their wishes. The hippie commune came closest to the way of life that could answer his current needs.

In therapy we worked out many problems he was having with his parents, including his acting out against them, and established that he really did want to achieve and that he was college-oriented. He found that when McCarthy and Kennedy came into the forefront and a part of the hippie group shifted into the Yippie political activist area he had a chance to join them and really do something about what his parents had been only talking about for so many years. Therapy helped bring to the surface his early identification with his parents' ideals. He could then move from this hippie refuge and re-enter college where he began to identify with college life from an activist's point of view. It is doubtful if therapy alone could have led him back to college as quickly as it did, were it not for fortuitous political events and social trends that enabled me to redirect him.

At our last meeting he was doing quite well in college and has since graduated. He still uses drugs, but the pattern is markedly different now. He smokes marijuana regularly and takes LSD once every month or so when pressures on him become very strong. But he controls the experience, the drugs do not control him. This is an important distinction to make in evaluating the potential harm of drug abuse.

Case 2: Alice was 16 years old when she ran away from home. Her father found her in the street by cruising the East Village, block by block. She had been taking every drug available except heroin. Her older brother, who was eighteen, was also somewhere in the East Village virtually out of touch with his parents. I learned a year later that he had become a heroin addict, but at that time he was very heavy into speed. The family lived in a New Jersey suburb. Both the mother and father were in therapy with the same psychiatrist. The parents were extremely status-conscious, living far beyond their means and, although presenting a good front, were actually quite miserable. Though fairly well-to-do, they were deeply in debt because of their chronic overspending. They were very active in local civic and social activities, belonged to several clubs and went out frequently. The father also worked long hours at his job establishing his own advertising agency and his work often kept him in Manhattan at night when he was entertaining clients. By chance, Alice found out that her father had been engaging in sexual experiences nightly when in town and that her mother knew about it but, for whatever reasons, ignored it and did not complain. At that point, it seemed to Alice that the kind of life they lived at home was a pure farce. There was little of positive value in the parents' relationship, but it served the mother's purpose to stay married because of her social standing in the community, and because divorce would have made her life less comfortable as she saw it. The father also found that for business purposes and other reasons, maintaining the marriage was convenient. His wife didn't give him any trouble and he didn't really want to get deeply involved with the women he was having relations with, so remaining married was a good excuse for him. It was a very unhealthy environment in which Alice and her older brother were growing up. The parents had no interest at all in the children. They focused on what looked right, rather than on what was right. They were essentially unemotional and were largely concerned with their own materialistic interests. They had very little use for political and social issues. Alice found herself completely isolated and extremely depressed. She took to playing rock music all night in her room (which she kept locked) and then was finally introduced by a friend to the East Village scene where she was turned on to drugs almost immediately. She found a new kind of life and a new freedom. She had friends, and decided that nothing else counted, certainly not school or home. She quit school completely (where she had been doing badly anyway) and decided not to return home. It was at this point that her father went into the Village, picked her up and brought her to me on the recommendation of his own therapist. We made a contract late that night that she would see me for a certain period of time, provided she did not have to live at home. We found a place for her to stay in the city while she was seeing me.

Drugs, with which she was now freely supplied by her Village friends, filled a great oral dependency in this girl. They produced feelings of euphoria and relief of depression, anxiety and tension. She expressed tremendous hatred towards her parents and then in another session complete indifference to what they cared about or what they thought. She wished that they were dead and declared that she did not care whether she ever saw them again. I could find no positive identification in the several sessions we had together. Among her hippie friends in the Village she was the baby. They fed her, they cared for her, they gave her a pet name, and she did not have to do anything at all, although occasionally she would panhandle just for the fun of it. Even in this activity, however, she seemed to be asking people to love her, to care for her, to pity her. She could not tolerate psychotherapy at all. I was unable to get her to face herself because the drug supports in the culture provided such immediate relief of tension, and depression that it was impossible for slow-acting psychotherapy to compete.

At last report, she was living in a commune with ten or eleven others. She never leaves the area at all. She is so safe in this particular four or eight block compound that she won't even go to mid-town for anything. She found a *home* which nurtures her and cares for her in somewhat the way a very benign state hospital would for a very regressed psychotic person. This girl was not psychotic, but for all intents and purposes she was socially psychotic. She was so immature and regressed, her dependency needs were so great, her frustration tolerance so low—only drugs satisfied enough of her needs quickly enough. The formal structure of psychotherapy and the confrontations and tensions that occur in a one-to-one setting just could not work for her.

The two cases are fairly typical of the middle-class family whose youngsters get involved in the drug scene. The ghetto youngster who becomes very involved with drugs is a different problem. One would have a difficult time reaching him in a one-to-one treatment. To begin with, the poor simply don't have the money to come to a psychiatrist. They don't have the sophistication to make use of traditional psychotherapy and their pathology is much more social and cultural than psychological. It is a way of life that needs to be changed and one can't do this by focussing exclusively on intrapsychic phenomena. What the ghetto youngster who is heavily into drugs has in common with the middle-class youngster on drugs is that they are both terribly disillusioned with life as it is; they are very unhappy. Whether it is depression which they are trying to overcome with drugs that are euphoria-producing, or whether it's anxiety, unhappiness and lack of hope for the future that drugs will take care of by offering an instant world of oblivion or fantasy, the fact is that the middle-class youngster who is heavily involved with drugs is just as pessimistic about his future as the ghetto youngster is. With the ghetto youngster it is quite easy to see why he is hopeless or greatly dissatisfied. He lacks equal opportunities for schooling, for jobs, and so on, but as seen in the two cases presented, the middle-class youngster who looks as if "he has it made" is no better able to follow the mode of life middle-class America offers and sees his way of life as a dead end too. The middle-class youth may see unhappiness, sterility and few spiritual values in the home. Yet his parents are deemed successful in this culture, so what can he do? Either run away from it with drugs or stay there and fight it. Very few young people have the kind of integrated personality, sophistication and wisdom or power to fight the entrenched power structure of middle-class society and its values. Running away, turning to drugs and forming their own society as hippies have done in their communes then represent alternate and experimental ways of living which they hope will be better.

For ghetto youngsters who have turned to drugs, the problems are quite different. One has to motivate the community to become a social force and a power so that the poor, the oppressed, the discriminated against develop better self-esteem and a measure of direction and control over their lives. This is extremely difficult to accomplish against a power structure which has spent many years developing the system we have today. People in the community who have been so powerless for so many years must realize that they can do something if they join together and cooperate and assert their rights. Leadership in New York's Lower East Side has not been strong, for example, and help from someone representing the middle-class power structure is looked upon with suspicion and often outright hostility. My own efforts to do something met with much resistance: What do I have in my mind as a white, middle-class, successful psychiatrist going into a black and Puerto Rican area and trying to stir things up there? I must have something in it for myself, they say. And I do. Certain gratifications and needs of my own, perhaps, but they are not nearly so malevolent as many blacks and Puerto Ricans feel they must be.

Encouraging these parents and adults to work together in some kind of cooperative enterprise, to realize that they can vote and change the local politics in the area, that they can do something about education and housing is essential treatment for the young people in the ghetto area. Take, for example, members of the Black Panther movement today. They don't use drugs. They don't use drugs because they are so committed and dedicated to improving and changing their life style that drugs would interfere with their efforts and compromise the work they are doing.

What one needs is an alternative to drugs where drugs seem the only way one can face life. An alternative is commitment to something in life that is important and that can be achieved. Bettering one's life and changing the status quo makes it possible to find new self-esteem, new status, a new expression of power and a realization of one's own potential that make drugs less important and less necessary. In the same way, the middle-class youngster who finds school not relevant to his needs and who finds that the life style he is falling into is not productive or gratifying, has to find alternatives. The hippie experiments, the drugs, the communal living, are the methods that these young people have used to find meaning in life, where they are at, what their values are, what's important and what isn't. Management of the ghetto and middle-class youngster on drugs then, may require a broad approach. He must be helped to find alternatives, opportunities, goals that can be fulfilled. There is nothing more frustrating for a black or Puerto Rican than to hear: "You know you can become President, if you only try." When he realizes that the opportunity that is supposedly there does not really exist he may, in his disillusionment and rage, find in drugs a way to both dissipate and escape from these feelings.

We have encouraged the community in the ghetto areas to become involved in the school system. School now is a middle-class structure which is not geared to the needs of the ghetto child who usually finds that he is not being taught anything useful. The Puerto Rican youth who frequently doesn't even understand the lesson taught in English, seeks an alternative to the boredom of school. If he quits school, he suddenly has six to eight hours a day, with nothing to do. With little chance for involvement in anything else there is much more time to get involved with drugs. If you don't have to study, if you don't have to do any homework for the next day, there is more reason to take drugs to fill the void. So, changing the school system to make it more relevant to the needs of the young people, is another important treatment step. Many of the middle-class youngsters who are on drugs tell me that they are terribly bored in school. Why are they bored in school? Well, they are being taught things that are obsolete and in any event not relevant to many of the crises we face today. It's one thing to teach Latin and ancient history in a very secure, quiet, happy time when one has the luxury to do things in a leisurely way. But society is changing so rapidly, and in so many ways, it is imperative that the system regulating our life—the courts, schools, and other institutions—also make changes to become relevant to the needs of a youngster. When this does not happen, the young become vulnerable to the solutions offered by the drug scene.

I would like to outline what I think can be done in treatment as it exists today. Family therapy is essential with the drug-using adolescent. In every instance I have seen of a youngster who *abuses* drugs, there is a family problem. Beyond the obvious factor of parental drug use, which a youngster can emulate and identify with, there may be tensions, hypocrisy, unhappiness and lack of communication which may propel a youngster into drugs as one

way of coping or adjusting. Opening lines of communication between parent and child is extremely important in the treatment
of drug abuse. So many youngsters do not tell their parents about
the drugs they use. Parents ask me (and as soon as they do, I know
that I will have trouble with them), "What can I do to find out
if my youngster is taking drugs? I really don't want to go through
his drawers and I don't want to go through his pockets because
I don't think it's right, but I really have to know, don't I?" I
would say: "No, you don't really have to know that way. If you
can only find out that way, it's not going to help you." I then explore this lack of communication and the trouble within the
family that leads to it. I frequently see the adolescent and the parents together and when I do the screaming and yelling can get
quite loud. However, I find this extremely useful because parents
and children then expose themselves in ways that they never do
when I see one or the other alone. Such family interviews can cut
through months of therapy and allow the physician to demonstrate
convincingly what the family members have been doing to each
other.

Getting the family involved is basic, and so is the education
of the family—teaching them what drugs are and what they are
not. I have never yet found a parent who was able to tell me in
a satisfactory way how he could justify his drinking alcohol and
come down so hard on his son or daughter for experimenting with
marijuana. The rationalizations such parents use are often extensive and compound the difficulty a therapist has in reaching
them. It is a rare parent who will say: "You know I understand
why he is taking marijuana and it really isn't any different from
my taking alcohol and I don't have any reasons to justify my doing
what I do and then condemning his use of a drug quite similar to
mine." Education has to be part of the treatment program. It
should not be attempted in one lecture or one talk because the
parents' defenses are just too strong. When I talk to P.T.A. meet-
ings about drugs and the parents' responsibility for the use of
drugs by the youngster, they never hear it the first time. They
tune out. But, if I can get them in groups three or four or five
times I find that they begin to respond and I can break through

defenses. Thus I find that an encounter or sensitivity group for parents can shorten the time necessary to cut through to their attitudes and biases about drugs, and enable them to talk about their problems with their youngsters and see where their difficulties really lie.

Group therapy for the adolescent is a way for a number of young people to get help with their drug problem. Group therapy with adolescents is more appropriate than with any other age group.

This is a stage in development when individuals naturally form groups, are much more comfortable in them, and rely on their peers for affirmation and support more than they do adults. In the group situation, drug-abusing youngsters can talk about their problems, share difficulties they have in living with their parents and parent culture, get support from each other and then work through problems in this supportive setting. They can more easily tolerate the tension of working through anxieties because of this support from the group. In short, the group therapy approach can be extremely helpful and often much more productive than one-to-one therapy.

For the ghetto youths addicted to heroin who need a residential setting, there is the therapeutic community which is, however, not designed for the younger adolescent. At Horizon House in New York City which is based on Synanon, Daytop and similar treatment centers, the average age is about 18½. The hard encounter group session works well with the older addict who has been an addict for about 10 to 15 years, who is a real manipulator, a real con-man, and who knows every trick in the game. The confrontation technique used can break down his defenses more effectively than any other technique we use. This method, however, is too rough for the adolescent. The therapeutic community structure is in many ways a brain-washing, behavioristic therapy in a 24-hour-a-day milieu. The basic ingredient is faith and total belief in everything the leader says. You follow the whole program, even if at the beginning you don't understand why, because eventually you will know why. For the older addict who has been an addict much of his life and whose addiction is a way of life, the need is for re-education and re-learning in a way that, perhaps, the therapeutic community can do best of all. But, the adolescent doesn't need so much re-learning and re-education; he needs education and learning for the first time. The kind of rigid structure that the therapeutic community provides is not good, in all its aspects, for the adolescent. Consequently, I would recommend a therapeutic community very much modified to meet the particular needs of the adolescent. There would be a psychiatric counseling service, a vocational and educational program including placement services, and with this a therapeutic community approach which would be a kind of mass group therapy, to give him the support that his own community and his parents have been unable to. Again, it is the style of life that needs changing, including social and cultural components which individual therapy leaves untouched.

A project in San Francisco called Number One takes youngsters who are very heavily into drugs or have other difficulties. They enter a house which is set up with different divisions. Within the house is an architect, a film-maker photographer and other skilled professionals and artisans. A youngster is screened and interviewed to find out what talent he has, or what potential. He is then directed to a tutor-teacher who has four, five or as many as ten youngsters working with him. The teachers then try to develop that potential. This then is another alternative to drug-taking—getting youngsters interested and involved in something that will stir some enthusiasm. Anything that promotes growth and development and increased self-assurance is potentially much more attractive to the teen-ager than drugs.

In summary, therapy will differ depending on the particular situation. The meaning of the drug to the adolescent must be ascertained and then appropriate steps taken to eliminate the need for it.

For the physician the family unit will still be his main concern and a study of the family structure and its functioning will often reveal the motivating forces for excessive drug taking. Working with the parents and the adolescent to provide corrective changes in their communicative and living patterns may be effective in many instances.

Concrete ways of offering help include pinpointing some constructive activity that appeals to the particular youngster and involving him in it.

Group therapy among the poor is often best conducted in a setting within their neighborhood, rather than in the doctor's office. The latter, together with clinics attached to hospitals, are representative of the feared and mistrusted establishment for some segments of the ghetto population and hippie or counter culture groups. When such feelings exist, the youth will not go for treatment and therapy must therefore be brought to him. Storefront operations and mobile trailor units have been used for this purpose in New York's Lower East Side and elsewhere.

The physician interested in working with such groups must in effect become a street worker. Those who have attempted it and survived the early frustrations, have found it a very rewarding experience. He must be prepared to deal with the politics that are increasingly becoming an integral part of the ghetto scene. He should have the special ability to relate to adolescents and to understand them. Speaking their idiom is not essential and often comes off as artificial, or even patronizing. It is more important to be oneself, candid and forthright. The gulf that exists is decreased if the professional worker has shared some of the experiences of the patient. This fact often makes the person who has himself used some of the drugs in question a more acceptable counsellor.

Most of the treatment approaches I have described can certainly be used by the family physician willing to expose himself and undergo some preliminary training. The majority are not able to do this and those who choose to continue operating within the traditional walls of the office, can still make an important contribution when confronted with a drug-using adolescent and his distraught family.

CHAPTER 9

A ROLE FOR THE FAMILY DOCTOR

MICHAEL G. KALOGERAKIS, M.D.

A T A TIME WHEN SPECIALIZATION in medicine seems to be reaching a point of no return, it may seem paradoxical to be giving thought to expanding the functions of the family physician into an area which one ordinarily thinks of as requiring highly refined expertise. The bulk of psychiatric knowledge is indeed much removed from the day-to-day concerns of the general practitioner, the pediatrician, the internist. Yet there is an important interface involving each of these disciplines and the field of psychiatry, and the foregoing chapters have explored this in some depth for specific areas of concern. I propose in this final chapter to review these interfaces and to consider in concrete terms how the physician equipped only with the psychiatric training he has received in medical school and during his internship can play a significant role in the short and even long-term management of the maladjusted adolescent.

The needs of society in these troubled days are enormous and cannot possibly be met by any single discipline nor, apparently, even by the collective efforts of all the professions traditionally concerned with psychological and social dysfunction. Thus we have arrived in the day of the paraprofessional, who is being systematically introduced into schools, clinics, community health centers and even in hospitals as a member of the mental health team with a distinct contribution to make. Just how this plan will ultimately work out is not certain but we are learning much from the endeavor.

The physician, whose primacy as mankind's clinician reaches back to the beginnings of history, comes naturally to the task of handling problems faced by the contemporary adolescent. If he is indeed the family's physician, he has the distinct advantage of knowing the family and the adolescent patient for many years, perhaps since the latter's birth. The extent to which he is now successful will depend on two major factors, highly variable from one practitioner to the next. First, his familiarity with basic psychiatric principles of diagnosis and psychodynamics and the current adolescent scene; secondly, personality characteristics such as sensitivity, patience and compassion.

In recent years, medical school curricula in the United States have strongly upgraded psychiatry as one of the major clinical sciences, on an equal footing with internal medicine and surgery in many medical centers. The National Board of Medical Examiners devotes an important segment of its examination to psychiatric issues. All this represents official confirmation of a view of psychiatry as having a wide application in all clinical medicine. Internships of whatever emphasis often include significant liaisons to psychiatric units and sometimes a specific rotation. Although exposure to adolescent psychiatry is still scanty, the current medical graduate is entering practice far better prepared than his predecessors to confront general psychosocial aspects of medical practice. Whether this is responsible for the observation that many young physicians seem more concerned with the broader social issues than any previous generation has been, or whether this is merely the medical version of a major return to humanism that can be seen among lawyers, educators and other professionals is difficult to say. In either case, it is a welcome development, one that bodes well for the future of medical practice in America.

For the less fortunate majority of physicians whose exposure to psychological medicine was often skimpy and of such inferior quality as to leave them uninformed and occasionally establish strong biases against psychiatry, a job remains to be done. Brief continuing education courses may be necessary and have in fact sprung up in many areas, often in response to an expressed need. The seminar or work-shop approach is to be preferred to the lecture, offering as it does the opportunity for real exchange and interaction aimed at undoing bias, at the same time that it seeks to impart basic knowledge and skills.

Most important is to provide a thorough picture of the current adolescent subculture in its various ramifications. The belief systems governing adolescent behavior may vary from place to place and certainly change with each generation. The current fashions and behavioral norms should be known as they are the context within which a given patient's problems must be viewed.

As to the personality characteristics enumerated, though they are of the essence in approaching the adolescent holistically, there may be little one can do when the physician lacks them. Often, such a trait as patience is lost in the whirlwind pace of a busy office practice.

The doctor whose practice includes much emergency work may find it impossible to take extra time for the psychiatric problem that is generally perceived as less pressing. An obvious solution if one wishes to work with adolescents is to restructure one's practice but this may pose some realistic difficulties, including the possibility of financial loss. It is a matter to be individually decided, of course, in keeping with one's changing interests and priorities. Physicians who have revised their practices have found the following useful:

1) Set one afternoon aside for adolescent appointments.
2) Initial appointments can be of usual length.
3) Use the examining situation to ask about school, home or dating—with experience a lot can be gotten out of 5 to 10 minutes by way of identifying a problem.
4) For the youth in need set up a return counselling appointment in late afternoon or evening.
5) Arrange with parents to charge on a time basis rather than visit basis.

This approach can be instituted with child and family as the former approaches adolescence.

Although the school remains the primary institutional locus wherein an adolescent is likely to be identified as requiring help of a general kind, it is to their physician that the average American family is likely to turn for most signs of disturbance that do not specifically relate to academic performance. Herein lies the most important fact for our consideration: the opportunity for effective intervention provided by the initial contact, an opportunity which must not be lost. The adolescent, frequently already convinced that the adult world cannot or will not understand him, seizes every chance to confirm his prejudice and the *occasion manqué* at the point that he yields and agrees to see the doctor may be all he needs.

Diagnosis

The presenting problem may often be physical though immediately suggesting a psychological basis. (One estimate is that 20 to 25 percent of an adolescent medical practice consists of psychosomatic problems). Once established that no medical treatment as such is necessary, the patient has often been dismissed with a statement (perhaps intended as reassurance) that "there's nothing wrong with you." In all fairness to the examining physician his has at least been an honest statement designed to spare the patient further expense. By thus missing the boat, however, the physician has forced many a frustrated adult patient to seek his cure elsewhere. The group thus turned away probably represents the greatest percentage of those making up the clientele of chiropractors and other would-be healers.

The harm done when the patient is an adolescent is probably much greater. His recourse may be to turn within himself or to seek relief via one of the methods currently in vogue among his peer group, e.g. drugs. The establishment, extension of his parents that it is, has failed him once more, and he is not likely to trust it soon again.

The options available to the physician who sees a patient with persisting symptoms, whatever their origin, are only two: to treat, if in his estimation he is able to manage the problem, or failing that, to refer. He must neither minimize nor disparage the symptoms presented by any patient he examines, however hypochondriacal or hysterical these may seem. Even the malingerer with a school excuse on his mind deserves a psychiatric evaluation (though he may refuse to cooperate). As always, the correct way to proceed can only be determined by a thorough diagnosis, which, in addition to the usual physical examination and laboratory studies, may require substantial exploration of the patient's life situation.

What are the important things to know, what areas need to be investigated? An adolescent may be self-referred, although more commonly an appointment has been made by his parents. He may be in acute distress or without visible discomfort. There is likely to be a difference in the nature of the problem faced by the physician depending on which of the four groupings thus formed the patient falls into. Some clues as to how to proceed might be derived from such an initial determination.

Perhaps the first task of the physician faced with an adolescent is to identify what the patient is *feeling* emotionally. This is best achieved by seeing him alone without the parents, clearly indicating that *he* is your patient and that you are not there to serve the parents, as well as emphasizing the confidential nature of whatever transpires.

Feelings associated with a visit to the doctor are generally quite few in kind. The adolescent in acute distress is apt to be experiencing one of the following:

(1) Anxiety or fear.
(2) Shame.
(3) Depression.
(4) Anger, resentfulness, hostility.

The feeling might be quite visible and easily identifiable. Not uncommonly, however, one may have to scratch the surface a bit and give some thought to the specific emotion being observed. Adolescents are so deeply concerned with "saving face" they are apt to conceal or mask feelings they equate with weakness. For example, a depressed mood may strike the physician as characteristic shyness or sullenness, anxiety as "typical adolescent hyperactivity." Such missed appraisals commonly lead to wrong approaches, failed diagnosis and ultimate loss of the patient. The adolescent relies heavily on others' ability to read his feelings without his having to spell them out. At the same time, he will generally cooperate in pinpointing the emotions if he senses the physician is genuinely interested and compassionate rather than judgmental. (It is always safe to say, "You seem kind of low," or 'You're very uptight today," as openers.) He may be able to say what he feels but be quite unable to relate it to anything in his life. In such cases, the cause and effect relationships are unconscious and dealing with them will be a more difficult task. It is here that systematic review of the vital areas of adolescent functioning—also the areas in which conflict is more likely to exist— should help identify the prevailing disturbance. These areas are listed below in an order that might easily be followed by the physician, the aspects of greatest interest being highlighted for each of these areas:

1. School—attendance, academic performance, general behavior, socialization.

2. Peer relations—are there any, are these only casual or are there deeper relations, is there a close friend one can trust completely, do friends include both sexes, are they patient's age? What is the make-up of the peer group and what activities take up their time?

3. Leisure activities—are there any, are they shared or solitary, how varied, are they stable or short-lived?

4. Adult relations—are these avoided or sought after?

5. Home situation and relationship to parents—easily the most important area though often resistant to exploration. It is best to assume that there is always *some* trouble, and work from there in tracking it down. Value differences pointing to a generation gap are more easily talked about than problems of parental discord, dependency, deeply felt hostility or the adolescent's own oppositionalism. Areas of *minor disagreement* (e.g. about clothes, curfew hours or household chores) may represent the visible part of the iceberg. Talking about friends' parents or the patient's siblings may be useful avenues that will lead ultimately to a quite candid discussion of his parents.

6. Sexual and romantic—has interest developed as yet, what is its extent, nature, what is the frequency of contact, how much gratification is derived from it. If engaging in genital petting or intercourse, does orgasm occur and how regularly?

Since, as already pointed out, the adolescent is much concerned with facesaving, how the questions are put will make a great difference in the accuracy or completeness of the reply. For example: "I suppose your parents argue, like all parents" rather than "Do your parents fight?"; "How often do you masturbate?" rather than "Do you masturbate?"; "When did you last see your best friend?" instead of accepting a general statement that "I have lots of friends."

Minors' Consent

Several important problems arise when the adolescent is self-referred and the parents are not involved. It is illegal to treat a non-emancipated minor in most states without permission of parents or guardians. The physician deciding to treat is consequently exposing himself to possible repercussions and even lawsuit. In actual practice there have been no court cases against a physician for counselling an adolescent on his own consent. In New York, a law recently enacted allows married 18 year olds to consent for themselves and their children. It also allows a physician to render emergency treatment without consent. However the most important service that can be rendered by a physician faced with an adolescent estranged from his family may well be to reestablish the dialogue between the patient and his parents, thus obtaining their consent for treatment. In many instances, notably the older adolescent who has left home and is living under more-or-less emancipated circumstances (e.g. the hippie in a commune), such a goal may be realistically impossible.

Yet medical and psychiatric care on the minor's own consent, at least initially, may be a frequent need. It is particularly for such youngsters that adequate covering legislation is necessary. The physician faced with a self-referred adolescent and unable to involve the parents is left to choose between running the risk of treating or turning the youth back to the street. In many instances of runaways seen in urban areas such as New York's East Village, especially among those involved in drug use, a general suspicion of public hospitals and clinics makes many choose to self-medicate, seek clandestine *medical* care or else to ride out their illness without medical attention of any kind. This has become a social and medical problem of major proportions and current solutions barely qualify as stop-gap measures. Many lay and professional groups actively concerned with issues of child and youth advocacy are seeking remedies using as many approaches as offer promise of help (e.g. medical, judicial, legal, philanthropic). The Joint Commission on the Mental Health of Children has published a lengthy volume spelling out detailed recommendations, including one for Advocacy Councils to be located within the communities across the land to handle medical, emotional and educational needs of children and adolescents. Enabling legislation has been proposed at the Federal level but thus far not been acted upon.

When To Refer

Before deciding to treat a particular adolescent, a doctor must screen out those patients who should be referred almost immediately. A number of determinations must be made:

1. Is it an acute emergency requiring immediate hospitalization? (a stat psychiatric consult may be advisable to confirm such a need.)

    —most grossly psychotic patients—exceptions are patients already known to the physician who are being maintained in the community.

    —acute drug intoxications with severe emotional disturbance (disorientation, delusions, depression, etc.) especially if medical pathology such as withdrawal phenomena is also present.

    —deeply depressed patients, particularly if unable to identify the source of the depression and when serious preoccupation with suicide coexists.

    —patients who have recently made a serious suicide attempt (to be distinguished from a *gesture*, whose goal is not self-annihilation but manipulation of others) ; more urgent if there have been a series of such attempts with evidence of increasing seriousness.

    —patients expressing deep concern over possible imminent loss of control that might endanger life or property.

—those without such *concern,* but having persistent homicidal thoughts or irresistible impulses; if already acted upon in some measure, such a condition is ominous.

2. Is the patient cooperative? Does he seem to be reaching out for help? The angry, resentful or very paranoid youngster may not permit an opening to the physician. The same may be true of the youth strongly committed to antisocial ways or heavily involved in drugs. He may not wish to change. However, such an adolescent may accede to the doctor's offer to intercede with his parents on his behalf. Such intervention could thus provide the opening wedge for involving the patient in the necessary course of therapy.

3. Is the patient already in treatment with someone else? If so, and regardless of whether the treating person is a physician or not, contact should be established to exchange information and consider whether some joint action may not be indicated. (Many physicians, perhaps because of lack of familiarity with the ways of other professions, are loath to call a psychologist or social worker.)

4. Does initial exploration indicate either a complex neurotic process or a serious personality disorder as the basis of the symptomatology, alteration of which would require too lengthy a commitment or specialized skills.

5. Similarly, is there a sense of immutable chronicity (as in a severe chronic schizophrenic) and no visible acute symptoms that might possibly be helped by occasional brief intervention (e.g. by psychotropic medication) ?

In all the above instances, the most important task of the family physician may be to adequately prepare the patient to accept and make use of the referral to a psychiatrist. The groundwork laid during the first contact may make the difference between the patient who follows through and the one who does not, as well as the willingness to trust the psychiatrist if he does keep an appointment. Generally speaking, an adolescent in acute distress will readily accept help from any corner. Occasionally, however, he may be afraid of the idea of seeing a psychiatrist. ("I must be really crazy") or mistrustful, viewing him as more a member of the establishment who wants to convert everyone to his way of thinking than he is likely to feel about the general practitioner. An opportunity to air such misgivings, a firm statement from the doctor that only the specialist can help in the particular instance as well as reassurrance that the psychiatrist is known to the referring doctor and is a *good person* should suffice to overcome resistance in most cases.

In referring to a psychiatrist, it is important to recognize that not all psychiatrists work well with adolescent patients. The physician's referral list should therefore contain at least one name of a person skilled in the area of adolescent psychiatry with established ability to relate to the teenage youngsters.*

Treatment

The physician is aware that treatment begins when the patient walks into the office, perhaps even from the moment he has made a decision to see the doctor. Benefits may already be accruing, depending on the nature of the problem. I should like in this section to take up the specific techniques that can be employed by the physician working with adolescents who has deciced against referral to a psychiatrist, at least as an immediate step. I shall also devote some comment to what therapeutic efforts are best avoided, except by the unusually endowed physician who may actually be equipped with psychiatric skills.

Among the techniques the physician can and selectively should use are the following:

Listening—the attentive ear, the compassionate tongue can accomplish a great deal in most situations. Often, it may be the first time an adult has been willing to hear out the troubled youth without censuring, preaching or seeking to dominate.

Clarification—the occasional question, interspersed in a talkative teenager's story will help focus the issues. When the patient is less garrulous (the monosyllabic variant is a classic), clarification will require a comprehensive series of questions phrased in such a way as to allow short and even nonverbal answers of assent or denial.

*The American Society for Adolescent Psychiatry keeps an up-to-date directory of its membership which can be obtained by contacting Mrs. Mary D. Staples, Administrative Secretary, 24 Green Valley Road, Wallingford, Pa. 19086.

Reassurance—here is where many a competent clinician falls flat on his face. Our own anxiety frequently drives us to offer reassurance at all costs, even when no solutions are forthcoming. To be successful, attempts to reassure must be scrupulously honest: it is far better to confess that you see no immediate solution to the problem than to engage in wishful thinking when the patient knows better. The most important reassurance is probably provided by the physician who by his *manner* convinces the adolescent that he will follow through and not let the matter drop.

Medication—here the physician is altogether on home ground as society's sole pharmacotherapist. The simplicity of the approach harbors many dangers. It may be resorted to unduly by the physician since it is far less time-consuming than the talking therapies. It may represent yielding to the patient's wish for a magical solution that requires no effort on his part. It may unwittingly encourage dependency on drugs, perhaps already a problem. Worst of all, since it generally addresses itself to relief of symptoms as a sole approach, it may totally ignore the causes of the troubles that have brought the youth to the office, perpetuating his problems by relieving his anxiety and interfering with his desire for a solution. As part of a combined approach, pharmacotherapy has a most important place in our armamentarium and can generally be easily managed by the family doctor.

In most instances of anxiety and tension, the milder tranquillizers (Valium, Librium) will provide sufficient relief. The phenothiazines are best reserved for very severe anxiety or agitation, as antipsychotics or for patients who may require or have already been in a hospital. Antidepressants have not been found to be useful with adolescents by this writer.

Intercession—usually with the family, but also with school, the police or the courts. A family conference, with the doctor presiding, may go a long way towards healing rifts and re-establishing the dialogue between parent and child. This can be a complex undertaking fraught with many risks and goals must be kept limited and clearly defined. First, the physician must be clear that his patient is the adolescent and that he is basically interceding on *his* behalf. Being clear about this in one's own mind and enunciating it for all interested parties to hear will help avoid the pitfall of unwittingly becoming the parents' emissary. Secondly, the doctor must rigorously steer clear of judgments about who is right and who is wrong in the over-all situation, particularly since both generations have certainly contributed. At the same time, this should not preclude open and honest but compassionate criticism of particular attitudes or actions of either side. Thirdly, the success of the opening foray will indicate whether further contacts should be attempted, whether a skilled family therapist should be brought into the picture, or whether this modality seems either unnecessary or unworkable.

Schools may need a physician's statement that there is an existing emotional problem which may require adjusting the student's program, providing special help or even granting temporary medical suspension.

The police are usually happy to have a doctor interested in a youngster who has run into trouble with the law and will often work together with him to help the youth. Here again, the understanding the physician can provide about the basis of the trouble often leads to more compassionate handling by the law.

Though Family Courts rely heavily on mental health professionals from many disciplines for most of their work, the family doctor who has known the patient and family for some time is in a unique position to help.

A word of caution: as general policy, it is not in the patient's interest to routinely *get him off the hook* when he is in trouble with the authorities. This tends to reinforce the antisocial pattern and further convince the youth that anyone can be manipulated and that the world is basically corrupt, thus providing solid rationalization for his own behavior. To intercede in such a way is destructive. To do so when the patient is not well-known to the physician or not to follow-up the case afterwards is consequently medically contraindicated as well as ethically wrong.

It is apparent from the foregoing that there is much the general physician can do. It is important to know what he ought not to attempt, and many a physician willing to deal with the emotional aspects of medical practice has expressed concern about where to draw the line, what limits to set for himself. The following brief suggestions may prove helpful.

Exploration in depth—Although some patients readily unfold their innermost thoughts almost on initial contact, this is more likely to occur with the most disturbed patients and is generally unusual in the healthier adolescent. In the normal course of development of neurotic processes, defenses are erected to protect the individual from painful ideas and wishes or from having to deal with unsurmountable conflicts. The clinician must remember that such defenses (repression, denial, rationalization, projection, intellectualization, etc.) would not be there were they not *absolutely essential* to the individual. They must therefore always be respected. What this means in practice is that we do not seek to penetrate too deeply beyond the conscious awareness of the patient. We deal with the material he presents to us, focussing on the immediate problem in as pragmatic a way as possible. The very disturbed (psychotic) patient who may launch into unconscious material straightaway and confuse and overwhelm his listener, must be stopped by constantly bringing him back to the current reality. Similarly, the less disturbed patient who attempts to involve the physician beyond the latter's capacity to understand or help must be discouraged. An honest admission that the doctor is not qualified to deal with such matters usually takes care of the problem. Though the bait is often dropped to draw us in, we must not take it, remembering that the immediate goals of our involvement seldom require it. Probing questions aimed at uncovering hidden motives are best avoided.

Interpretation—In contrast to clarification and confrontation which deal with *conscious* material, this technique, the cornerstone of psychoanalytic treatment, attempts to account for otherwise incomprehensible behavior and irrational thoughts on the basis of *unconscious* material that emerges gradually as a patient talks and as it appears in his dreams. Skillfully used, it is our most valuable tool for altering well-established neurotic patterns or personality dysfunction. Unfortunately, it is often misused and every psychoanalyst has seen the results of unwarranted interpretation or wild analysis on patients who come to him after they have been in treatment elsewhere. The well-trained analyst relies heavily for his interpretations on the patient's own associations and does not permit himself too much freedom in interpreting dreams, symbols and fantasies from his own associations.

Is this a technique that can safely be used by the general practitioner? It is here, I think, that the line can be clearly drawn, for interpretation of unconscious materal is the province of the analytically-trained professional. It requires a profound knowledge of the psychology of motivation and psychoanalytic theory as well as the trial and error experience of supervised analytic work. The clinician, even if a psychiatrist, who has not had the benefit of a thorough personal analysis is unable to know with certainty the extent to which his own unconscious processes either blind him or distort his perception of the patient's problems. He may honestly believe he is serving his patient. He may actually be placing him beyond the reach of even the highly skilled professional for, even in trained hands premature interpretation often leads to intellectualization and other defensive operations which can then become entrenched and serve as effective barriers to the development of further insight.

Behavior modification—A variety of techniques are subsumed under this rubric including operant conditioning, desensitization, positive reenforcement, aversive conditioning, etc. In many ways, these are familiar and commonly applied aspects of normal child rearing and other human relations. Although they are therefore easier to apply then interpretive techniques, to be used systematically and effectively they also require specialized training. This may sometimes be available in post-graduate courses with highly specific goals (e.g. antismoking) but someone who lacks such training should not attempt to apply the techniques. It is unlikely that the family physician will encounter much opportunity to use such approaches in his work with adolescents, whose problems generally call for some combination of the techniques outlined above.

I have reviewed some of the problems of working with an adolescent population as seen by the psychiatrist. I have tried to

convey my conviction that there is an important, largely unful-
filled, role that the general physician can play in this work which
can be very gratifying to the doctor and of crucial value to his
teenage patient. Perhaps the major difference between the exclusive concern for the physical problem presented and this ex-
panded approach into matters both social and psychological is that
the physician as a person, his beliefs, attitudes, prejudices, his
hopes and frustrations, all become part of the doctor-patient interaction. This may not be desired by some but is sure to be
welcomed by others. From his end, the adolescent desires it. He
wants to be in touch with the adult as a total person and is made
uncomfortable by the non-reacting approach that has been the
hallmark of much psychoanalytic work with adult patients. With
adolescents, involvement is often inevitable and, for the doctor,
carries an important responsibility which bears re-emphasizing.
The physician cannot, on the one hand, allow his personal moral
values to interfere with his professional judgment. At the same
time, it is difficult to be other than what he is. His politics, his
religion, his deep convictions about child-rearing, about a child's
role in society and particularly with regard to authority—all are
and remain part of him. He can even own up to his differences
with his adolescent patient, as long as he recognizes, in a tolerant
and compassionate way, his patient's right to be himself, to differ,
to seek new solutions.

The physician must be aware of the great power he wields,
both realistically—where he must use it constructively and chari-
tably—and psychologically, where he becomes willy-nilly an important role model for many an adolescent, all the more so if the
patient's parents have failed to effectively execute their primary
function in this regard. As role model, his every word, his every
action carries tremendous potency, a power we may often wish we
were not given. We cannot wish it away, we can only be keenly
aware of its existence and sensitive in our use of it. Nor should we
be dismayed when the power the adolescent has invested us with
is suddenly and summarily withdrawn, for no apparent reason.
Omnipotent yearnings left over from our own childhood make us
vulnerable to rejection, push us to take on more power than we

should, and at other times cause us to deny the power that we appropriately possess.

The troubled adolescent is today one of society's greatest challenges. To the clinician who has chosen to work with this age group, he is a source of much frustration, confusion and even turmoil. As if by magic, he seems to engender in us the same feelings he is himself struggling with. Therein lies perhaps his greatest appeal. He forces us to re-examine our own frequently outmoded ideas, he touches our sore spots and ruffles our feathers. Our honesty and integrity are thrown open to question. Our complacency is buffetted and the ground underneath seems suddenly less firm. Many a physician has told me how he has grown through his work with adolescent patients. Perhaps the contact with ever-changing youth serves also to keep us young. All this added to the contribution we are able to make towards tomorrow's world in laboring with today's heirs makes it eminently worthwhile. The creative physician able to tolerate some dislocation of a traditional office practice will reap rich rewards in an exciting and significant endeavor.

NAME INDEX

Abraham, K., 64, 69
Agras, S., 55, 69
Alexander, F., 31, 44
Anthony, J., 59, 70
Arieti, S., 82

Balser, B., 68, 70
Beck, A. T., 52, 70
Bender, L., 68, 70
Bibring, E., 64-65, 70
Bierman, J., 54, 70
Blaine, Graham B., Jr., 79
Blender, L., 82
Bleuler, E., 72, 82
Boulanger, P., 64, 70
Bowlby, J., 54, 70
Bruch, H., 40, 44
Burks, H. L., 58, 70

Campbell, J. D., 59, 70
Cobb, Stanley, 33, 44
Cornelison, A. R., 83

Daniel, W. A., 21
Day, J., 83
Despert, J. L., 54, 70
DeYoung, C., 83

Eisenberg, L., 73, 82
Engel, G. L., 31, 40, 44, 54, 70

Finesinger, J., 70
Fleck, S., 83
Flomenhaft, K., 83
Freedman, A. M., 82
Freud, Sigmund, 64, 70, 73, 82

Gallagher, J. R., 21
Gallagher, Roswell, 3
Goldfarb, W., 53, 70

Gould, Robert E., 92
Greenacre, P., 70

Hammer, S. L., 21
Harms, E., 36, 44
Harrington, M., 55, 70
Harris, H. I., 31, 44
Harrison, S. L., 58, 70
Hassan, J., 55, 70
Heims, L., 70
Hill, O.W., 57, 70
Hirsch, S. I., 83
Hoch, P., 71
Hofmann, Adele, D., 3
Holterman, V., 21
Howells, G. S., 44

Jacobziner, H., 67, 70
Joffe, W.G., 54, 65-66, 71

Kalogerakis, Michael G., 106
Kanner, L., 52, 70, 73, 82
Kaplan, D.M., 83
Kappelman, M. M., 21
Kasanin, J., 58, 70
Kaufman, I., 58-59, 70
Kaufman, M. R., 58, 70
Keller, W. R., 70
Klein, M., 64, 71
Klerman, G. L., 52, 71
Kraepelin, E., 72
Kremer, Malvina, W., 46

Langley, D. G., 83
Lehmann, H. E., 52, 71
Lidz, T., 83
Ling, W., 56, 63, 71
Lorand, S., 45

123

SUBJECT INDEX

DATE DUE

DEMCO 38-297